Praise for *Set Free to Ch*

Josh McDowell is a man who knows the truth and shares it with authority and power. He is a gifted writer who has helped me in my walk with Christ, and now he has created a new tool that will help every parent teach the toughest truths and discuss the most difficult areas of life. I love how he shares his own struggles and his own insights on victory. I have shared this material with my own kids, and it has provided us with new ways to say yes to what is right and how to do the next right thing. You will love *Set Free to Choose Right* if you love teaching your kids how to live the Christian life.

—Stephen Arterburn, Founder and Chairman of New Life Ministries

Any book Josh McDowell writes is worth much more than the price of the book—and this book is no different! Josh offers parents Jesus-focused instructions on parenting leadership and very practical direction on pursuing an intimate relationship with our kids based on love and transparency. The Bible and real life illustrations show how raising our children by living out Jesus' instructions on leadership really work at home. This very valuable and usable book will equip any parent to lead their kids with love!

—Barry St. Clair, author, speaker,
and President of Reach Out Youth Solutions

In a world where distractions permeate every screen and Wi-Fi signal, today's parents need to teach their kids truth so they are equipped to recognize lies. In these pages, Josh helps us segue from high guidance to setting our kids free to choose right. I'll definitely be recommending this book in my parenting workshops.

—Jonathan McKee, President of TheSource4Parents.com,
speaker, author of *If I Had a Parenting Do Over* and
The Teen's Guide to Social Media & Mobile Devices

Social media tempts us to think that staying in constant contact with our kids is enough. In reality, they need deep trust, not just frequent touches. Josh takes the reader on a very personal, humbling journey of how to develop that kind of relationship with our kids. *Set Free to Choose Right* comes at exactly the right time for me as a dad, and at just the right moment for our culture.

—Jeff Myers, Ph.D., President of Summit Ministries

I appreciate that the biblical principles and practical insight in Josh's book *Set Free to Choose Right* have been forged on the anvil of real life experience. This book is a very helpful guide for parents and caring adults in guiding young people to embrace biblical convictions in today's foggy moral environment.

—Daryl Nuss, Executive Director/CEO of
National Network of Youth Ministries

After three decades of working with families and students, I have found no better resource than Josh McDowell. His consistency and drive to hit the big issues is something to be admired. Once again, Josh is tackling the definitive issue for our children, how to say yes to God's best. I believe in today's world there is a battle for the hearts, minds, bodies, families, and futures of our young people. *Set Free to Choose Right* fillets this issue down to the bone. This is a must read!

—Dr. Jay Strack, President and Founder of Youth Pastor Summit
and Student Leadership University

Set Free
to
CHOOSE
RIGHT

Equipping Today's Kids to Make
Right Moral Choices for Life

JOSH MCDOWELL

SHILOH RUN PRESS
An Imprint of Barbour Publishing, Inc.

Print ISBN 978-1-63409-974-5

eBook Editions:
Adobe Digital Edition (.epub) 978-1-68322-673-4
Kindle and MobiPocket Edition (.prc) 978-1-68322-674-1

Published by Shiloh Run Press, an imprint of Barbour Publishing, Inc., 1810 Barbour Drive, Uhrichsville, Ohio 44683, www.shilohrunpress.com.

Our mission is to inspire the world with the life-changing message of the Bible.

ecpa Member of the
Evangelical Christian
Publishers Association

CONTENTS

ACKNOWLEDGMENTS

I wish to recognize the following individuals for their valuable contribution to this book.

Dave Bellis, my friend and colleague for over forty years, for collaborating with me on the outline of the book, pulling from my other works to then write the first draft, folding in all the edits, and shaping this work into its final form. I recognize Dave's writing skills and insights on the subject matter, and I'm deeply grateful for his contribution.

Tom Williams, for editing the manuscript to which he applied his valuable insights, wordsmithing skills, and passionate heart to help make these words come alive on the printed page.

Becky Bellis, for laboring at the computer to ready the manuscript.

Jake Kissack and Ben Bennett for reviewing the parent/child interaction in the fictional story and providing excellent input in order to make the story more realistic.

Jessie Fioritto, for the editorial guidance she brought to the manuscript's completion.

Kelly McIntosh, vice president of editorial at Barbour Publishing, for her expert insights and help in shaping the direction of the book.

Tim Martins, president of Barbour Publishing, and the entire Barbour Publishing team, who caught the vision for this book and the Set Free Journey and labored tirelessly to launch this book to the Christian community.

–Josh McDowell

CHAPTER 1

What Were You Thinking?

*I*t was a little past 10:30 p.m. when Aubrey Jefferies slipped quietly into her home. The PTA board meeting had droned on much longer than she anticipated, and she hoped her husband, Brad, had not waited up for her. The lights were turned off, so she assumed that he and their two teenage children were already in bed. Guided by hallway nightlights, she tiptoed up the stairway and down the hall, hoping she could slip into bed without awakening her husband.

As she made her way past the bedroom of Jayden, their fourteen-year-old son, she thought she heard a muffled sound coming from under the closed door. She stopped to listen. It sounded like the voice of a woman. Aubrey slowly turned the doorknob and peered into the room. Jayden was sitting at his desk with his back to her, staring intently at his computer. Displayed on the screen was a provocative young woman, completely naked, speaking to the viewer in seductive tones.

"Jayden! What are you doing?" Aubrey blurted as she stepped into the room.

The startled boy slammed his computer shut and turned wide-eyed toward his mother. "I–I was just. . . It–it's not what you think, Mom," Jayden stammered.

"Don't lie to me, young man," Aubrey retorted as she flipped on his bedroom light. "I saw what you were doing." She stepped back into the hallway. "Bradley," she called, "come to Jayden's room—right now!"

In a matter of seconds, Brad was in the room facing his wife, her voice approaching a shriek, and her finger jabbing the air toward their son as she explained how she had caught him viewing internet porn.

"Dad, it wasn't like that," Jayden protested. "I was just doing some school research, and I just happened to. . ."

"You were researching naked girls for school?" his mother interrupted. "I don't think so!"

"Okay, okay, let's chill a little." Brad motioned with his hand for Aubrey to calm down.

"Jayden, are you saying you weren't on a porn site?"

"Yeah, no—I mean, I was just—uh—doing some research for my homework, and I came across this site and didn't really know what it was until I. . ."

"So you admit it, you were on a porn site!" Aubrey interrupted.

"Okay, okay!" Jayden countered. "I may have ended up on a site like that, but it's not that big a deal. Come on, Dad, you know how it is."

"Bradley!" Aubrey looked straight at her husband. "What does he mean, 'you know how it is'?"

Brad hesitated, took a deep breath, motioned for his wife to back off, and spoke directly to his son. "You and I have talked about the dangers of porn sites before, Jayden. There's a lot of bad stuff out there." Jayden, feeling like a cornered animal, stared at his feet. "Look at me, son," Brad said in a soft tone. "Have you been getting into this stuff?"

"No," Jayden protested.

"Let me see your computer." Brad reached out for his son's laptop. The boy reluctantly handed it over.

Brad quickly checked the computer history. He slowly shook

his head as he looked at his wife and then back to his son.

"You're lying, son. You've been doing this a lot." Brad's voice clearly conveyed his disappointment. "Whose credit card have you been using?"

"Credit card?" Aubrey responded. "You mean you've been paying for this slutty stuff!"

"Come on. Whose card, Jayden?" his dad insisted.

Jayden stared at the floor and in a low voice said, "Mom's."

"You've been using my card to visit porn sites?" Aubrey's voice rose with each word. "Shame on you, Jayden Allen!"

Brad shook his head slowly. "What were you thinking, Jayden? You know this isn't right. We've taught you better than this."

"Okay, okay!" A touch of belligerence edged Jayden's voice. "I'll pay you back for the credit card charges, but I don't see why you're making this into such a big deal. Everybody does it, and I'm not hurting anyone."

What Makes Right Choices Difficult

Like Brad and Aubrey in the above story, we all want our kids to resist temptation and make right choices. We try to give our kids wise counsel, teach them what is morally right and wrong, and hope they follow through and do the right thing. Yet it has become increasingly more difficult to lead our kids to make right choices. It's not that parents, grandparents, pastors, youth workers, and Christian educators aren't desperately trying. Today more than ever, gatekeepers of youth are running scared that our increasingly ungodly culture is drawing our kids away from biblical moral truth.

No doubt you have felt that fear. There is no denying that we face an uphill battle, but it is a battle that we can definitely win. In spite of formidable competition from our pervasive culture, it is still possible to instill biblical morality within your kids that will govern their choices. But to do so we must come to grips with at least three critical issues. To empower our kids to discern right from wrong, we need to squarely address a *cultural issue*, a *child development issue*, and a *parental methodology issue*. Confronting and understanding these issues will lay the solid foundation from which we can set our kids free to choose right.

1. A Cultural Issue

In our story, Jayden's parents considered viewing internet pornography to be morally wrong. But Jayden excused his behavior because to him it was no big deal. His perspective on the issue was that he had the right to judge for himself whether internet porn was wrong for him. He did not see it as that bad because, as he said, "I'm not hurting anyone." He saw it as a private issue that did no harm to either him or to anyone else. So why should it be considered wrong?

Jayden's view is representative of an entire generation of young people who believe that right and wrong are determined by the individual and not by any absolute standard. Many believe they have the right to decide for themselves what is right and to act accordingly. The belief that one can choose his own morality without suffering consequences or hurting anyone is erroneous, as we shall soon see.

Scripture warns us over and over of the consequences of becoming our own arbitrators of truth. This view that truth is relative and individually determined arose in the Garden of

Eden and caused the downfall of our primeval parents. It was the prevalent cause of Israel's seesaw history and ultimate collapse. The entire book of Judges provides us with a quintessential example of what happens when a society determines its own morality. It chronicles the devastating results of moral relativism upon a nation. When the people of Israel judged for themselves what was right and wrong, they began to experience severe social dysfunction. Families suffered moral breakdown. Civility was soon abandoned. Theft, violence, and lawlessness became pervasive. The last verse of the final chapter of Judges sums up the cause of the whole problem: "In those days Israel had no King; all the people did whatever seemed right in their own eyes" (Judges 21:25). In other words, moral relativism became the rule of the day, and the cohesiveness of the nation fragmented into rampant individualism.

It is moral relativism that sets the human conscience adrift. It allows the heart and mind to excuse attitudes and behavior that are wrong and harmful to oneself and others. Young Jayden gives us a typical example. In his mind, viewing internet pornography is no big deal. He has formed his own, privately held moral principle that removes pornography from the sin list. He is like 68 percent of teens and young adults in America who don't believe viewing pornographic images is wrong for them.[1]

And it's not just our teens. Think of the people you work with and the neighborhood in which you live. Do these people believe there's a universal moral code to follow, or do they think right and wrong are relative—to be determined by the individual?

While studies show that 80 percent of Americans express concern about the nation's moral condition, 57 percent of your neighbors and coworkers believe truth is relative and that right and wrong are subjectively determined by the individual.[2] And if your neighbors are Millennials (those born between 1984 and 2002), 74 percent of them believe morality is "whatever seems right in their own eyes."[3] These polls express a strange paradox: while Americans are acutely aware that the morality of the nation is declining, they are oblivious to the fact that the slide is caused by their own moral relativism. As a famous cartoon character of the past used to say, "We have met the enemy and he is us."

Among the most alarming factors that play into this issue are the schoolteachers that have authority over your children for six or more hours every day. Do these adults believe there is a truth that is right for everyone or that truth is situational and whatever works for the individual is what is right for that person? It pains me to say that the vast majority of our nation's teachers have been indoctrinated in moral relativism throughout their college years. Duke Pesta, professor at the University of Wisconsin—Oshkosh, makes this astute observation about today's relativistic educational system:

> *It starts at the top, in the journal articles and published books that secure tenure and impose the ideological dictates determining the construction of curricula and the way we train teachers from kindergarten through high school and beyond. At the highest levels of academia, the tenured professoriate— and the professors, deans, provosts, chancellors, and university presidents who almost always arise from the privileged ranks of this tenured class— there exists a dangerously monolithic echo chamber, where relativistic, post-modern ideas about the*

world, culture, and truth have become calcified. The consequences to education of this ideological conformity can be witnessed at every level of public, and in many cases private, instruction, for many private schools only hire teachers trained and certified by state-run education programs.[4]

Consequently, from the start most teachers view all learning through the lens of moral relativism. Count on it, if your child is in public school, and perhaps even in some private/Christian schools, he or she is being influenced to believe that right and wrong are to be subjectively determined.

Twenty-five years ago, a major TV network news anchor reported that a significant number of students cheated on their tests and that professors knew that cheating was widespread. This finding was alarming enough, but something even more appalling within that report really caught my attention. The news anchor went on to explain that the majority of the students that cheated *did not believe there was anything wrong with it.*

That news report, in part, led us to commission a study on morality among teenagers within Christian families and solid Christian churches. Subsequently, we wrote a book that included a full analysis of that study. That book—*Right from Wrong: What You Need to Know to Help Youth Make Right Choices*—is still in print after two decades, and the book you are now reading is a companion to it. (See epilogue for more information on that book.) Back then, 71 percent of kids from Christian homes believed that moral truth was subjective and individually determined.[5] And the percentage holding that viewpoint has remained constant over the past twenty-five years.

In the pages that follow, we will demonstrate how this relativistic view shows up in your child's world, where it comes from, and how to counter it effectively. Helping your young people redefine the culture's view of truth, especially in the area of sexuality, is a critical step in the process of helping your kids learn to make right moral choices.

In today's highly sexualized and hedonistic culture, much of our moral concerns for our kids do center on sexuality. Almost every facet of society pushes our young people toward sexual immorality. God's way, as we know, leads us in the opposite direction. Paul puts it this way: "We must not engage in sexual immorality" (1 Corinthians 10:8). So leading our kids to make the right moral choices sexually should take high priority in today's cultural climate—not only because it is biblical, but for another reason as well. Lead your kids to make right choices regarding sexuality, and the other guidelines and commands of God will tend to fall in place. Why? Because living pure and faithful sexually encompasses so many other important values in life, including honesty, self-control, respect, love, loyalty, responsibility, trustworthiness, integrity, patience, honor, unity, and intimacy.

Our sexuality touches on much of who we are and how we relate to one another. Help your young people make the right sexual choices, and they will also learn much about what it takes to form and maintain healthy relationships. So our running story at the beginning of each chapter will largely be dealing with choices relating to a young person's sexuality.

2. A Child Development Issue

In our story, Jayden paid for his visits to internet porn sites with his mother's credit card. How could he think he wasn't going to get caught? Didn't he know that the charges would show up on Aubrey's credit card bill? Did he think she wouldn't notice? It's no wonder Brad asked his son, "What were you thinking?"

The answer is that Jayden was not thinking rationally at all. He was not connecting the dots into a composite picture of his actions and their consequences. In fact, he, like virtually all teenagers, is developmentally incapable of making consistent sound, rational thoughts and decisions. Why? Because the decision-making part of the adolescent brain is not yet fully developed. Twenty-five years ago, neuroscientists believed the adolescent brain was as fully matured physically as the adult brain. But through "brain mapping," medical scientists have found that the decision-making part of the brain—the prefrontal cortex—isn't fully developed until a person reaches his or her twenties.[6]

To complicate matters, the limbic system of the adolescent brain, where raw emotions are generated, is in a stage of high-powered rapid development. Dr. Robert Sapolsky, professor of biology, neurology, and neurosurgery at Stanford University, puts it this way: "In an adult, the frontal cortex steadies the activity of parts of the limbic system, a brain region involved in emotion; in contrast, in the teenage brain, the limbic system is already going at full speed, while the frontal cortex is still trying to make sense of the assembly instructions."[7]

What this means is that teenagers' emotions are developing far ahead of their rational thinking. This occurs because the prefrontal cortex in teenagers is not fully mature, and it limits to some degree their ability to make consistent sound decisions, especially under the pressure of volatile emotions. The more-developed, highly active limbic system is like a busy highway crowded with speeding cars. The less-developed frontal cortex is like a traffic signal that doesn't always work correctly. Sometimes it flashes from green to red without hitting yellow. Sometimes it is green in all directions at the same time, prompting emotional pandemonium. Researchers suspect that this imbalance between the two systems keeps teenagers from tracking multiple concepts and inhibits them from gaining instant access to critical memories and thoughts that are necessary components in making consistent sound judgments or controlling unruly emotions.

Imagine your teenagers with a limbic system running at freeway speed, primed to react instantly to anything that might endanger their turf, such as a disagreement with you over fashion, friends, music, or even the viewing of internet porn. With their prefrontal cortex on emotional overload, teenagers don't always have the brainpower to organize their thoughts and make sound decisions. This biological reality has been recognized by the US federal government and has been instrumental in shaping laws to protect adolescents, primarily because they have not fully gained a developmental sense of decision making. In 2005, the US Supreme Court ruled that the death penalty is unconstitutional for juveniles, stating that "parts of the brain involved in behavior control continues to mature through late adolescence."[8]

This isn't to say that teenagers are devoid of a conscience or shouldn't somehow be held accountable for their actions. But it does explain why our kids are prone to wrong choices that seem to make sense to them at the moment. The good news is there are powerful steps you can take to offset the underdeveloped reasoning center of your child's brain. You can help your kids to better navigate through the teen years and still make wise choices—and we will explain how in the later chapters.

3. A Parental Methodology Issue

The information you provide your kids, the guidance you give, and *what* you say to them are all important. But just as important, or even more so, is *how* you convey this information. How you relate to your child personally is critical. I have often said, "Your kids won't care how much you know until they know how much you care."

We can lay down all the rules in the world and make every effort to enforce them. But unless our kids know with their heads and feel with their hearts that those rules come from the loving heart of a father and mother or caring youth worker, they won't be highly motivated to obey them or even listen to us, regardless of how diligently we enforce them. Biblical moral truths must be placed within the context of a loving relationship if they are to be passed on effectively to the next generation. And that requires engagement in a continual process.

God told the people of Israel to commit to obeying His commands and to impart them to their children. They were told:

> *Repeat them again and again to your children. Talk*
> *to them when you are at home and when you are on*
> *the road, when you are going to bed and when you*
> *are getting up. Tie them to your hands and wear*
> *them on your forehead as a reminder. Write them*
> *on the doorposts of your house and on your gates.*
> *(Deuteronomy 6:7–9)*

Transmitting God's moral values to your children requires a repetitive process. The word *repeat* in Deuteronomy 6 is the Hebrew verb *shaman*, which suggests engraving or impressing words onto a surface so it cannot be obliterated. The idea is to keep at it until God's ways are indelibly impressed into the hearts and character of our children. In fact, when you consistently and lovingly impress God's ways upon the hearts of your children, you are in a real sense setting them free to choose right over wrong.

In the chapters to follow, we will share with you a simple but profound four-step process you can repeat over and over again to your children. It is a process in which every moral value God has given can be passed on. It is straight out of scripture, powerfully effective, and as relevant as this morning's sunrise.

That may sound simple, and it is; but it's not easy. It takes dedication to your kids and a commitment to God's ways, but it will work. Yet I find that even dedicated parents have their doubts. I've had them come up to me with all the dedication and commitment in the world and lament that they simply can't compete with all the outside influences that tug at their kids. They say things like, "Josh, my kids are inundated by the media—iPhone, iPad, YouTube, texting, tweeting, Facebook, Netflix, and school. They're learning everything from everyone but me. I don't stand a chance!"

A lot of parents feel that way, but they're dead wrong. With all of today's technology, social media, and all the distractions your kids face, you are still the most important and most influential figure in their lives.

A national online study shows that 45 percent of young people consider their parents to be their role models.[9] I suspect you thought today's musical sensations or young movie stars or sports celebrities were your kids' role models. But they're not. Other studies show that 32 percent of today's kids look to their friends and just 15 percent look to celebrities for guidance and inspiration.[10] In fact, the studies show that even until your children reach twenty-five years of age, the greatest influence on their behavior will be the loving, close relationship with their parents, especially the father.[11] Researchers at the University of Florida recently stated that "the good news is that most teens ARE listening to what parents are saying despite what they [the parents] think."[12]

Your kids are watching and listening. You need to be armed with what to say and primed as to how to say it. You need a parenting methodology that is biblically centered. You need to navigate your adolescents' developmental process to shape their moral character effectively. And you need to know how to defend the truth against a culture that wants to capture your kids. All this is possible. God is there for you. And "if God is for us, who can ever be against us" (Romans 8:31). With dedication, commitment, effective tools, and God's help, you can instill God's moral values within your kids to "live clean, innocent lives as children of God, shining like bright lights in a world full of crooked and perverse people" (Philippians 2:15). And we hope the pages that follow will provide you with the challenge, encouragement, and tools to do just that.

CHAPTER 2

Who's to Say Who's Right?

When we left Jayden and his parents in the first chapter, tensions were high. Brad and Aubrey were just coming to grips with their shock that their son had been viewing internet pornography, and they were deeply concerned. But they were more concerned with the cavalier manner in which he brushed it off:

"Okay, okay!" Jayden felt cornered, and a touch of belligerence edged his voice. "I'll pay you back for the credit card charges, but I don't see why you're making this into such a big deal. Everybody does it, and I'm not hurting anyone."

"Jayden," his dad replied, "I know you think you're not hurting anyone by visiting those sites, but Son, this is a pretty big deal."

"Just how often do you view that trash?" Aubrey chimed in sharply.

"Come on, Mom," Jayden retorted. "Can't you lighten up a little bit?"

"Calm down, Son," Brad responded. "Your mother and I are just trying to figure out how deeply you have gotten into all this and how we can help you."

"You don't want to help," Jayden replied bitterly. "You just want to put me down."

"We don't want to put you down," Aubrey said in a softer tone. "We're just concerned about you. You've gone against what we've taught you. I mean, you do know that porn is wrong, don't you?"

"Yeah, I know it's wrong for you and Dad," Jayden responded. "But it's not that wrong for me."

"What do you mean, 'wrong for you and Dad'?" Brad asked. "This is wrong for everyone. We're talking about objectifying women, lust, immorality—you name it. Pornography is wrong, period, Jayden!"

"You guys are just too uptight," Jayden responded. "I mean the movies you and Mom go to are just as bad. I don't know why you're making such a big deal about all this. And anyway, I..."

"Okay, I see we're not getting anywhere with this," Aubrey interrupted. "It's late; we're all tired and a little upset, so let's just call it a night. Your father and I will discuss what to do next and how long you're going to be grounded. But from now on, you won't be using your laptop without going through me. I'll control the password!"

Different Standards

Fourteen-year-old Jayden clearly sees the issue differently from his parents. Visiting internet porn sites is no big deal to him; yet it is a big deal to his parents. Jayden and his parents reflect the divergent attitudes toward pornography prevalent among teenagers and adults today. This fact is confirmed by a major study.

In 2016, we commissioned the Barna Group to survey nearly 3,000 US teens, adults, church youth, and senior pastors on their perceptions concerning pornography and their use of it. The result was published as a study titled *The Porn Phenomenon—The Impact of Pornography on the Digital Age*. We have included a significant portion of that study in the appendix of this book.

The study confirms that our young people do not hold to the same standards on the issue of pornography as do many adults. Only one out of three teens and young adults consider viewing pornographic images to be wrong. In fact, our young people consider not recycling to be more offensive morally than viewing porn. While 56 percent cited not recycling as morally wrong, only 32 percent cited viewing pornography as morally wrong for them.[1] Additionally, our young people have a cavalier attitude toward viewing internet pornography. When discussing porn with their friends, 90 percent of teens and 96 percent of young adults say they do so in a neutral, accepting, or encouraging manner.[2] Given the fact that pornography embodies characteristics Christians have historically known to be wrong—the objectification of women, lust, the condoning of immorality, and the pull toward addictive behavior—it is imperative that we ask why the majority of our kids now consider viewing internet pornography to be morally acceptable.

The answer is that strong cultural forces have pulled many of our kids away from the moral teaching of their Christian parents. The dominant thinking of today's culture has led them to believe that the determination of right or wrong is basically a personal decision. They feel that a person has no right to judge what another does on the privacy of personal devices. They no longer believe there is a universal standard for sexual morality beyond a person's own view as to what is right or wrong for him personally. An astounding 70 percent of American young people today fail to embrace the concept that there is a universal standard for what's right or wrong. They have subscribed to the morality of the dominant culture. This is clearly demonstrated in the fact that 65 percent of all Americans of all age groups do not believe there is a universal standard for truth.[3]

Young Jayden's view of morality allows him to do essentially anything he wants sexually as long as it doesn't hurt anyone. T is also the majority view of adults today. Sixty-nine percent believe that "any kind of sexual expression between two consenting adults is acceptable."[4]

A Pew Research Center study found that 65 percent of Americans believe that premarital sex is acceptable. Perhaps the most startling factor here is that 36 percent of those surveyed don't even think sex before marriage is a moral issue. The same study found that 58 percent of the population endorses homosexuality as a valid lifestyle, with 35 percent of that group failing to see it as a moral issue.[5] One respondent summarized this view when she said, "If you want to poll attitudes toward homosexuality that is one thing, but don't couch it in terms of morality."[6]

These findings show that the majority of Americans see overarching, universal moral standards as meaningless, especially when applied to sexual issues. The only valid sexual moral standard widely endorsed today is the one you personally decide works best for yourself. That perspective is reflected in offhand remarks like: "No one has the right to impose his or her moral views on me; I decide that for myself." "How you choose to live your life is up to you, no one has the right to judge you." "That may be wrong for you, but it's not necessarily wrong for me."

Only Partially True

It's easy to see why deciding what is morally right for yourself would catch on and become so widespread. It puts *you* in the driver's seat. It feels good to make your own choices without moral police looking over your shoulder. No one wants to live under constant scrutiny and judgment. Shouldn't we have the right to make up our own minds about what is right for us personally? Didn't God Himself give us that freedom in the Garden of Eden?

There is a germ of truth in that viewpoint. God did give humans the right to choose their own way. And once that choice was made, God allowed it to stand. But this fundamental truth has been distorted and applied in a way it was never intended—as people tend to do to justify choices that are at odds with God. Yes, we have the freedom to choose whether to follow right or wrong, but we do not have the freedom to choose the *content* of right and wrong. And choosing wrong, even if we convince ourselves that it is right, does not exempt us from the inevitable consequences of our choice. This is where most of our young people and many others suffer from deep-seated confusion. That confusion revolves around the difference between the concepts of *truth* and *beliefs*. There is a vast difference between what one may believe *personally* and what is true *universally*.

Clearly, we are each entitled to hold our own beliefs, but that doesn't mean that we are each entitled to create our own respective truths. Truth must conform to reality, which means by its very nature it is independent of our beliefs. Beliefs, on the other hand, are essentially personal, and they may or may not conform to reality. One may hold a belief based on erroneous data that later information proves to be false. Or, as we will explore below, there are neutral areas of thought and action where universal truth need not intrude, and in these areas, making decisions based on opinion and personal belief is appropriate. But in areas where truth is defined by God, it makes no sense to say that something is true for you and not for me. Either that "something" conforms to God's universal standard for truth or it does not, and if it does not, then no amount of believing it to be true will make it so.

For example, imagine that you and your friend see a green apple lying on a table. Your friend believes its insides are rotten and full of worms. But you, on the other hand, believe it to be crisp and worm-free. Can your opposing beliefs about the apple create two distinct realities that are contradictory yet equally true? No. The two of you can subjectively believe what you want, but there is only one objective truth about the inside of the apple. The only way to determine that truth is to slice open the apple and observe the reality of its inner condition. Then you will discover the real truth about the apple—whether or not it has worms. The instant the apple is sliced, the objective truth will be revealed and the false belief will be exposed. The truth about the apple exists independently of the beliefs of either you or your friend.

Just as the truth about the apple exists independent of one's beliefs about it, the truth about right and wrong exists independent of anyone's beliefs about it. There are very specific and particular truths that exist independent of Jayden, his parents, and all of us. But while one can easily determine the truth about a concrete object such as an apple, the truth about an intangible moral principle such as sexual morality may not be so immediately obvious, especially to a generation bombarded continually by sexual stimulation from entertainment, advertising, education, and the media. So how can a generation skeptical of universal truth discover the independent and unchangeable truth about sexual morality?

All human beliefs have a source. The primary way to determine the validity of a moral truth is to look for that source. Did it come from human thinking and experience or some mesmerizing political demagogue or a famous philosopher or sage or prophet? If so, where did he get the idea? Human-made concepts of truth rise and fall with the times and are inevitably swept into the oblivion of history. But for morality to be authentic and universal, it must have a source beyond the human mind—a source that rests at the base of all sources—a source that is self-originating, self-existent, and has no source of origin but itself. The only source that fits that requirement is God. God has defined the truth about sexual behavior in His Word for all humans. That means the truth about sexual morality is universally true for all people for all times and in all places, and it is not subject to change based on anyone's personalized belief. God as the creator of humans laid out the terms of sexual behavior: He designed sexual relations to be expressed between one man and one woman within the exclusive bonds of marriage. To experience sex outside that boundary is to adulterate or contaminate the sexual experience. Scripture teaches that engaging in sexual behavior outside the exclusive nature of marriage makes sex impure or adulterated. That's why sex outside of marriage is called adultery.

Jesus said, "You have heard the commandment that says, 'You must not commit adultery.' But I say, anyone who even looks at a woman with lust has already committed adultery with her in his heart" (Matthew 5:27–28). Scripture goes on to say, "Put to death the sinful, earthly things lurking within you. Have nothing to do with sexual immorality, impurity, lust, and evil desires" (Colossians 3:5). That kind of moral truth is not up for consideration. It is not a matter of Jayden deciding whether it's right for him. It's not an issue of personal choice that one can modify or reject in favor of a morality more conducive to one's personal wants.

To clarify an issue that we noted briefly above, God does allow His people to adopt personal beliefs in some areas that are legitimately matters of opinion. It's what some have called "personal convictions." In the book of Romans, the apostle Paul addressed the fact that some Jewish followers of Christ were conflicted over what eating restrictions to follow, what festival days to observe, and on what day to celebrate the Sabbath. He told them that these decisions could be made individually on the basis of preference or conscience, and then he went on to warn that "those who don't eat certain foods must not condemn those who do, for God has accepted them" (Romans 14:3). Addressing what day a person should worship on, he said, "You should be fully convinced that whichever day you choose is acceptable" (Romans 14:5).

Paul was making the point that there are issues outside the universal moral law of God that required a personal decision—a decision that God accepts even though it may differ from the decision of a fellow Christian. I know some people who feel strongly that to honor the Lord's Day they must refrain from buying products on Sunday. Some people are convinced that to enroll their kids in public schools is wrong; they must either be educated in Christian schools or homeschooled. God allows freedom to make such choices based on personal convictions. The apostle Paul made this point quite clear when he referred to the Jewish regulations concerning what foods were pure or impure: "I know and am convinced on the authority of the Lord Jesus that no food, in and of itself, is wrong to eat. But if someone believes it is wrong, then *for that person* it is wrong" (Romans 14:14, emphasis added).[7]

The point is, God has given us certain universal truths. On the other hand, he has given us areas of choice in which we may form our own beliefs and do whatever works best for our situation or convictions. But when a culture treats universal truths from God as if they were malleable personal beliefs, it twists the truth into an error. We are free to determine our personal convictions on a variety of issues, but moral truth lies beyond one's personal determination. God has already defined that.

Defining the Standard of Truth

Someone has said—accurately, I think—that all disagreements come from differing assumptions. Jayden worked from the assumption that he had the right to decide whether viewing internet porn was right for him. As far as he was concerned, it wasn't even a moral issue. His parents, on the other hand, worked from the assumption that God had established the truth about sexual morality, and that lust is a violation of that truth. They determined, therefore, that pornography is morally wrong because it stimulates lust.

Had Jayden been required to make a "truth statement," it would be that he had the right to choose whether internet porn is right for him based on *his standard* of morality. Brad and Aubrey's "truth statement" would be that viewing internet porn is wrong for everyone, based on *God's standard* of morality. It really comes down to determining which standard is the correct one—which should be applied when faced with moral choices. Understanding the definition of truth helps us to make this determination.

Webster defines truth, in part, as "fidelity to an original or standard." To illustrate what this means, let's assume you and I are talking together when a stranger approaches and asks, "What time is it?" You look at your cell phone and say, "It's 2:23 p.m." But I look at my watch and say, "No, it's 2:26 p.m." Whose claim is true, yours or mine?

We could argue all day about whose device is the better timepiece. But to determine the correct time, we would have to compare the times shown on our devices with the international standard by which all world time is measured. That standard is set by the prime meridian, which is the longitude that runs through Greenwich, England, and is thus called the "Greenwich Meridian." That is home to Greenwich Mean Time (GMT). The day's date changes when the sun rises on that meridian. GMT is *world time*, and it is the basis for setting every time zone around the world. Although GMT has been replaced by *atomic time* (UTC), it is still widely regarded as the official measurement of time around the globe.[8]

So, if you and I want to establish which of our "truth statements" about time is in fact true—your 2:23 p.m. or my 2:26 p.m.—we would simply compare the times shown on our devices against the "original or standard" of timekeeping in Greenwich. Whichever of our claims about time is in accord with GMT will give us the truth about the correct time.

When we search for the "original or standard" for moral truth, we find it in God. Basing our claim on sound, solid, and testable biblical principles, we confidently assert that Creator God is the original and the universal standard for all moral truth. It is God who defines what is right, good, and true. Anything that does not conform to His standard is wrong, evil, and untrue.

Neither Jayden nor his generation can create their own moral truth. That truth cannot be individually created because it already exists in God as revealed in His Word. The task of Jayden's parents—and of us as well—is to lead our kids to discover God's truth. We must help them realize that the standard for moral truth doesn't lie within ourselves; it exists independently outside ourselves and in fact resides in the Holy One who created us.

The culture that is presently influencing our kids does not look to God as the original and standard for all moral truth. In this respect, today's culture is quite different from that of America's past. The second paragraph of the Declaration of Independence, in part, reads: "We hold these truths to be self-evident, that all men are created equal, that they are endowed by their Creator with certain unalienable Rights, that among these are Life, Liberty and the pursuit of Happiness."

Somewhere along the way, America abandoned its original foundation and no longer looks to God as the source of moral truth. Why and how did we as a nation lose our dependence on God? The answer to this question will give us insight into how we can reestablish that dependence within our homes and churches.

From Generation to Generation

It is not that the majority of our kids today are nonreligious; it's not that they are rejecting God. They are very spiritually minded, and most believe in God and the Bible. It's just that they feel it's okay to define God and shape truth differently than their parents do. It's not that they don't have a set of values—they do. The problem is that those values and morals are personally shaped by their own self-constructed standards. Truth and morality are therefore relative, situational, and personally defined.

You didn't lead your kids to think like that, which raises the question, who did? Where did they get their relativistic approach to truth? The thoughts, ideas, and beliefs that influence how we view the world don't simply pop into existence. The personal approach to determining truth that is dominant in America today is merely the current link in a historical chain of changing thought. It will help us know how to correct the moral relativism our kids have adopted if we familiarize ourselves with how attitudes toward truth have evolved from generation to generation to produce the current moral climate of the West.

God, the Beginning and the End—Ethical Theism

For centuries in Western culture, the starting point for all truth and morality was God as revealed in scripture. Life and death and the meaning of human existence were understood in the context of the universe as created and governed by God.

For some thirteen centuries after Christ, the acknowledged purpose of science and philosophy was to discover more about God and His design for humanity. The recognized end of all human effort and creative activity was to honor God. Art, literature, music, and architecture were intended to reflect God's glory. The acknowledgment of an infinite, almighty God made sense of the whole of human experience and provided the proper foundation for questions about right and wrong. But all that began to change some seven hundred years ago at the end of the period we call the Middle Ages. And that gradual change has brought us to where we are today.

The Renaissance Period

Beginning in Italy in the 1300s, great strides were made in literature, learning, art, and architecture. This period of European history is called the *Renaissance*. It stretched over the course of two centuries and spread throughout Europe, lasting through the sixteenth century.

Writers and artists such as Petrarch, Boccaccio, Giotto,

and Michelangelo sparked an era of extraordinary human accomplishment. The Renaissance also marked a significant shift in human thought. While the major focus of art, literature, and philosophy during the Middle Ages had been on glorifying and serving God, the Renaissance artists and thinkers began to exalt man and his abilities as the standard of all accomplishment. This shift gave birth to a doctrine called *humanism,* which stressed human dignity and ability. God was not yet eclipsed; most of the paintings of the Renaissance period depicted biblical events and much of the architecture was glorious and enduring cathedrals. But God's glory was often diluted as the artists themselves were often revered as much as their work. Renaissance thinking opened the door to regard man as the center of all things, the master of his fate, the captain of his soul. This emphasis led eventually to an unbiblical view of humans and their relationship to the Creator. As this way of thinking began to take hold, men and women's dependence on God as a source of truth and morality began to wane.

The Renaissance may have had minimal impact on human thinking had it not been followed promptly by the next period.

The Enlightenment Period

This period, which began in the 1600s and lasted through the next century, was also referred to as the Age of Reason. Enlightenment thinking advanced the idea that individuals have the right to reason for themselves. It's true that humans are rational beings with not only the right, but also the responsibility to exercise their God-given reasoning capacity. But the problem with Enlightenment thinking was that it tended to elevate reason above divine revelation. This was done, in part, as resistance to the religious superstition and dogmatism prevalent at the time. People began to feel free to determine what they believed on their own, independent of God and His Word.

While the Renaissance mind acknowledged God, many leaders of the Enlightenment, such as Voltaire and Rousseau, claimed that if there were a God who had created the world, He had no contact with it now. This meant that men and women were left to discover truth on their own by the power of reason; they could expect no help from God. Thus, standards determining right and wrong were no longer based on God and His Word, but on human reasoning. In the Renaissance, humans (not God) became central; in the Enlightenment, human reason became transcendent. The error of the Enlightenment was not in recognizing human reason as a wonderful thing (which it is); it was the attempt to crown human reason as king in God's place.

This laid the foundation for the present-day thinking that the individual has the right to determine his or her own truth. If that approach to truth is valid, then no one has the right to judge the morality of another. Once the transcendence of individual reason was firmly enthroned within culture, it set up three more periods that have brought us to where we are today.

The Industrial Revolution

The Industrial Revolution was an explosive period of human ingenuity and productivity. It overlapped much of the Enlightenment period, extending from the 1700s through the 1800s. Feeling empowered to think for themselves, people were motivated to unleash their creativity. The inventions, innovations, and improvements of the Industrial Age fueled more than factory furnaces; they stoked the fires of human confidence. The progress that men and women saw all around them encouraged them to look to themselves for hope and guidance. People no longer felt such a need to look upward (to God); they needed only to look inward (to themselves). With freedom of expression, entrepreneurship, and economic prosperity, much of society was led to conclude that their potential was limitless. This human-focused perspective all but pushed God out of the picture, except for the recognition that He was, of course, our Creator. That too would soon change.

Darwinism

The momentum of the Industrial Revolution was still in effect when the theories of Charles Darwin, a former theology student, completed the seismic shift that the Renaissance had begun. The publication of Darwin's *The Origin of Species* in 1859—which introduced the theory of evolution—had a profound impact worldwide. His theory presented an alternative to the theistic understanding of origins; God was no longer needed to explain or understand how the world and humans came to be.

This shift in thinking could now lead men and women to believe that they—not God—were the arbiters of truth and morality. Human reason had replaced God as the object of modern man's worship. Human accomplishments had fueled an arrogance and confidence in one's ability to create good and judge evil. Finally, with the publication and increasing acceptance of Darwin's theories, God became unnecessary and, in the minds of many, left individuals free to judge truth and to reach their own conclusions about right and wrong independent of God and His

Word. Friedrich Nietzsche took that line of thinking to its logical conclusion and, just prior to the dawn of the twentieth century, proclaimed that God was dead.

Modernism

The previous eras set the stage for Modernism, the age of unprecedented scientific achievement. It was during this period that the world heard these incredible words: "One small step for man; one giant leap for mankind." Science had put humans on the moon. Twentieth-century modernists began to see all the world through the eyes of science. This led Western culture to begin placing its faith in rationality and empiricism, the belief that objective knowledge can only be gained through our senses and evaluated by our minds. Any truth that cannot be observed and experienced—such as spiritual or moral truth—is to be considered subjective and must not be elevated to the position of objective knowledge. Since the standard for right and wrong cannot be apprehended through experience or the senses, the natural conclusion is that morality is solely dependent on what people feel inwardly is right or wrong for themselves. Lacking any standard for morality that can be experienced by the senses, one is free to formulate his or her own standard by integrating sensory data with personal preferences. In its simplest form, this method can be characterized in this way: "This feels good. I like it. I perceive no harm in it. Therefore, I will call it right for me."

Jayden and most young people today have adopted this modernistic thinking. Remember Jayden's response when his mother asked, "You do know that porn is wrong, don't you?" His answer: "Yeah, I know it's wrong for you and Dad. But it's not that wrong for me." Jayden is simply reflecting the way of thinking about truth and morality that has been institutionalized within our culture. Moral truth is not something you can scientifically observe and measure. And if pornography, premarital sex, or extramarital affairs can't be scientifically proven to be wrong, then we are left to decide subjectively if it's right or wrong for ourselves. That makes perfect sense to an entire generation.

Postmodernism—the Digital Age

In nonscientific areas, the effect of Modernism has devolved into a sort of foggy, roiling intellectual void commonly called Postmodernism. Jayden's thinking is representative of this extension of Modernism in that it separates the scientific from the spiritual, placing the former in the realm of absolute, verifiable knowledge and the latter in the realm of personal determination. Young people today are not relativistic when it comes to matters of science, engineering, and technology. Those fields deal with observable reality, producing results that are objectively verifiable. But when it comes to matters of religion, ethics, and morals, which make claims that cannot be verified by data apprehensible by the senses, young people treat those areas as subjective and relegate them to the realm of personal choice. They assume to themselves the authority to decide what kind of morality is right for them.

We now live in the Digital Age. It is a time of explosive growth in technology, massive dissemination of information, and giant steps in medicine and science. There is a growing belief among this generation that advanced science and technology are the only sure disciplines that can actually explain the world we live in and transform it for good. This makes human ingenuity and technological advancement our only hope for the future. So, we have no need to look to anyone or anything else to save us.

What Do We Do?

It is likely that your young people view God, the Bible, morality, and the values you are trying to teach them through this post-modern lens. This means they are working from a set of assumptions as to what is morally right and wrong that are totally different from yours. As long as they retain that working premise of moral relativism and the corresponding assumption that they decide for themselves what is right and wrong, nothing is apt to change. They will continue to adopt a process of mixing and matching the kind of God, morals, and religion that makes sense to their subjective feelings. That, of course, is highly troubling to those of us charged with our young people's spiritual welfare.

The pervasiveness of the postmodern philosophy makes it seem that the very foundations of moral law and order for our families and nation are crumbling. King David's question is as relevant today as it was when he penned it some three thousand years ago. "The foundations of law and order have collapsed. What can the righteous do?" (Psalm 11:3). The question cannot be more pointed. What can we do right now to build or rebuild a more solid moral foundation for our families and churches?

King David went on to direct us to the answer:

> The LORD is in his holy Temple; the LORD still rules
> from heaven. He watches everyone closely, examining
> every person on earth. (Psalm 11:4)

God is still there as the definer of true morality. He hasn't changed; He still watches and cares for this generation. The problem is that this generation is not seeing Him clearly for who He is. The secret to getting our families and churches on a firm foundation for making right moral choices is to lead them to a fresh revelation of the one true God. Many of our young people do not see God for who He truly is, nor have they experienced Him as their definer for all that is right and wrong. Changing that perception is definitely doable. We need not resign ourselves to the inevitability of our children being shaped by their culture. But they can still be shaped by God and His ways. In the following chapter, we will begin to share a process designed to rebuild the crumbling foundations of a universal morality based on God. By following this process, you can restore in your young people the power to make moral choices with God and His Word as their standard for truth. Read on!

CHAPTER 3

Right for a Reason

Both father and son were painfully aware of the leaden silence that hung between them as Brad drove Jayden to his band competition. Finally, Brad spoke.

"I know this isn't easy for you, Son, but your mother and I. . ." Brad glanced over at Jayden. He was fixated on his phone, his thumbs dancing over the keyboard at lightning speed.

"Can you put your phone down so we can talk?"

Jayden finished his text and sighed deeply. "Okay, whatever."

"I know you think your mother and I don't trust you anymore, but—"

"Yeah, because you don't," Jayden blurted.

"Hold on now, let me finish. What I was going to say is that we really want to trust you. We just need to know you're on the same page with us."

"Dad, you're never around long enough for me to even get on the same page with you. And it's impossible to get on the same page with Mom—she hates me."

"Now, Jayden, that's just not true. Sure, I'm gone a lot. It's my job, and it can't be helped. And your mother certainly doesn't hate you. She's just a little disappointed with you."

"You think?" Jayden responded sarcastically.

"What I'm trying to get at is that your mother and I would like to know that you understand that visiting those porn sites is wrong. That would go a long way toward rebuilding trust."

"I understand that you say it's wrong."

"But Son, it's not just me. The Bible says it's wrong. You're going against what the Bible teaches."

"The Bible says to love people and not to hurt them, right? What I've done hasn't hurt anyone, so I don't see why you're making it into such a big deal. But anyway, I've already told you that I won't go on those sites again. So why can't that be good enough? Why can't we just drop the whole thing?"

Why Are Some Things Wrong?

Brad and Aubrey want their son to understand that he has done something wrong. Even if he agrees not to visit porn sites again, they don't want him to excuse his misbehavior. They realize it is important for him to understand that he has done wrong. If our kids understand the wrongful nature of a given action, it can be a deterrent to repeating the offense. That's a good thing.

But even more important than knowing a given action is wrong is understanding *why* it is wrong. Brad, for example, would love for Jayden to understand what makes viewing internet pornography wrong. He would like for him to realize how lying about it to his parents is equally wrong. But simply stating that these things are wrong because the Bible says they are doesn't help him to reach that goal, for reasons that we shall soon see. The problem is that Brad, like many parents, does not know how to communicate to his kids why certain things are right and others wrong.

During my talks on the subject of knowing right from wrong, I often pose two questions to the audience about an act that people recognize as wrong: lying. I generally ask a teenager, a parent, and a youth leader or pastor to join me on the platform. I ask each of them two questions about lying, and here are the typical responses I get:

"Do you believe lying is wrong?" I ask the teenager. The answer is always, "Yes."

"Why do you believe lying is wrong?"

There is always a pause. Then the answer is generally, "I don't know. I guess I've just been taught it's wrong."

I ask the parent, "Do you believe lying is wrong?"

"Yes."

"Why do *you* believe lying is wrong?"

The parent generally responds, "Lying is wrong because it's being dishonest. And it's not right to be dishonest with people."

I press a little further: "Okay, what makes dishonesty so wrong?"

A pause, and then the parent asserts, "Well, dishonesty just isn't right. It can hurt people and relationships, and that's not right."

I move over to the minister. "I assume you too believe lying is wrong?"

"Sure," the pastor responds.

"Why?"

"Lying is wrong because the Bible clearly teaches it is wrong," the pastor declares confidently.

"Why does the Bible teach it's wrong?" I continue. "Well, oh… it teaches it's wrong, uh. . .because it's wrong." Typically the response is every bit that fumbling and uncertain.

I thank the three for participating in my little survey, and they go back to their seats. Then I explain that on the surface, each answer given was true: lying is wrong. But it isn't wrong simply because we've been taught it's wrong. It's not even wrong because dishonesty hurts people or damages relationships. Those are the negative consequences of lying. What I'm about to say next may alarm you, but hear me out: Lying isn't even wrong because the Bible says it's wrong. The Bible declares certain actions and attitudes such as lying, cheating, stealing, murder, adultery, and other behaviors to be wrong. But that declaration itself isn't what makes them wrong. There is an even deeper and more elemental factor that makes right, right and wrong, wrong and that factor is the very essence and character of God Himself.

God Is What Makes Right, Right and Wrong, Wrong

There once was a man described as being "after God's own heart." His name was David, the second king of ancient Israel. Yet as spiritually oriented as David was, he committed some terrible wrongs. He lusted after another man's wife, Bathsheba, and committed adultery with her. When Bathsheba became pregnant, David called her husband, Uriah, home from battle to cover up his sin. When Uriah failed to visit his wife, David ordered his general to place the man at the front lines of the battle where he was certain to be killed—and he was.

It seemed that King David had succeeded in covering up his sins until the prophet Nathan came to him and told a very moving story. Nathan reported that there was a rich man and a poor man who lived in a certain town. The rich man had many sheep and cattle. The poor man owned nothing but one little lamb. The little lamb was a pet that grew up with the poor man's children. It ate and played with his family. Nathan went on to say that the poor man even "cuddled it in his arms like a baby daughter" (2 Samuel 12:3).

One day a guest arrived at the home of the rich man. To

celebrate, he wanted lamb chops on the menu for his special guest. Of course, all he needed to do was serve up a delicious meal by roasting a sheep from his own large flock. But instead, he went out, took the dear pet lamb from the poor family, killed it, and served it to his guest.

David's reaction to this story was exactly like yours and mine would be. He was outraged! How could this rich man be so horribly selfish? How could he be so unfeeling as to take a poor man's pet lamb away from his children and kill it? It was all so unnecessary. The rich man had plenty. There was no need to selfishly take from someone in need when he himself had so much.

Then Nathan lowered the hammer on David. He said, "You are that man!" (2 Samuel 12:7). Immediately, the king grasped what he had done. He saw his sin for what it truly was—first and foremost an offense against a loving God who had so richly provided for the king. It was then that David made what some see as a startling confession. He said, "I have sinned against the Lord" (2 Samuel 12:13).

Why did he say he had sinned *against the Lord?* In the whole sordid event, he had created quite a lineup of wrongdoing—lust, covetousness, adultery, deceit, and murder. But each of these sins seemed to be solely against specific people. He had lusted after a woman, sinning against her. He had coveted another man's wife, sinning against him. He had committed adultery, a sin against both the husband and his wife. Then he had tried to deceive the people by covering up his deed, thus sinning against the nation he was charged to lead uprightly. And lastly, he intentionally had the husband killed, again sinning against Uriah with irrevocable finality. Yet in spite of the fact that all his sins were committed against specific people, David saw his true offense as being against

God. What did he mean by saying that?

We begin to see the answer in the message from God which the prophet went on to deliver to David:

> *I gave you your master's house and his wives and the kingdom of Israel and Judah. And if that had not been enough, I would have given you much, much more. Why, then, have you despised the word of the LORD and done this horrible deed? (2 Samuel 12:8–9)*

God took David's offense personally. He, the Great Provider, had given David everything he needed. But instead of being grateful and continuing to trust in his Provider God, David selfishly took what didn't belong to him, just as the rich man in Nathan's parable selfishly took the poor man's only lamb. That's what selfishness does. Rather than trusting in God's provision, it takes what doesn't belong to it. All sin is selfish and does what the prophet Nathan said David had done: "You have shown utter contempt for the Lord" (2 Samuel 12:14). Sin, which is derived from selfish attitudes and actions, is in effect showing disregard, disrespect, and contempt to a loving God who is our provider and protector.

By nature, "God is love" (1 John 4:16). God is perfect and righteous. "He is the Rock; his deeds are perfect. Everything he does is just and fair. He is a faithful God who does no wrong; how just and upright he is!" (Deuteronomy 32:4). God is holy and unselfish; He is giving and kind. Our sin is an affront to His righteous nature and caring heart. When we act contrary to the holy and loving nature of God, we can know our action to be wrong because it shows "utter contempt for the Lord."

Scripture reveals to us the essence and attributes of God. We are told that He is perfectly holy (Isaiah 54:5; Revelation 4:8), that He is love (1 John 4:16), that He is just (Revelation 16:5), and that He is right (Psalm 119:137). These are not things that God *decides to adopt*; they are what He *is*. All that is right and holy and just and good is derived from God's core nature—His essence. Scripture says, "Whatever is good and perfect comes down to us from God our Father, who created all the lights of the heavens" (James 1:17).

It is the nature and character of God that defines truth and thus enables us to determine what is right and what is wrong. It is the person of God that reveals what is right for all people, for all times, in all places. That is why we can assert with confidence that there is a universal truth, and that whatever deviates from that truth is wrong. Because the basis of everything we call moral—the source of every good thing—is the eternal God who is outside us, above us, and beyond us.

Many parents think as Brad and Aubrey do: certain things are wrong simply because the Bible speaks against them. Internet pornography is wrong because the Bible speaks against lust. Jayden argues from a socially construed perspective that porn is not wrong because it is a private activity that harms no one. Yet the bottom line is that internet porn and all sexual immorality is wrong because it is an offense against a loving God. He is hurt whenever we sin. It breaks His heart. The reason some things are right and some things are wrong is because there exists a Creator God who is not only righteous and holy, but is brokenhearted when we fail to trust in Him and follow in His ways.

Some things are "fair" and others "unfair" because our Maker is a *just* God.

Love is a virtue and hatred a vice because the God who formed us is a God of *love*.

Honesty is right and deceit is wrong because God is *true*.

Chastity is moral and promiscuity is immoral because God is *pure* and *faithful*.

So many of our kids can't distinguish between truth and error, between what's moral and what's immoral because they are not glimpsing the loving heart and character of God. He is the original, the standard for what is right and wrong, and thus the standard for all of our behavior in every area of life.

Pointing to the Person of God

When Dottie and I were raising our four children, we made a practice of having discussions on what made things right or wrong. For example, when I came home after a speaking tour, I would often take one or two of my children out for breakfast. As I drove to the restaurant (or while we were all munching on our bacon and eggs), I would suggest a situation in which we might be called on to make a moral choice. I would ask my kids questions to learn how they would decide what course of action to take, based on God's law that emanates from His character. The idea was to challenge their thinking and lead them to discover that morality rests in God's holy nature.

First, we had to determine what law or commandment from God applied to the particular situation I had constructed. But the important thing was to see how that law actually originated within the character of our holy God and how it reflected a given aspect of His love and care for us. My purpose was to acquaint my children with the kind of God we serve, not just the kind of laws we follow from the Bible. Dottie and I saw that our task as parents was to instill in our kids a foundation for evaluating, on an objective basis, why certain actions are morally right or wrong. It all boils down to whether the action reflects or contradicts the character of God.

I remember having a conversation with my then fifteen-year-old daughter, Heather, sometime after 9/11 in 2001. I asked her if she believed the Al-Qaeda terrorists who had flown the planes into the World Trade Center in New York City were morally wrong.

"Of course they were wrong," she said, looking at me as if I was crazy.

"Why were they wrong?" I asked.

"Because they killed all those innocent people," she answered with a sense of bewilderment as to why I would ask.

I explained that I too believed it was morally wrong, but I wanted to explore more deeply with her why it was wrong.

"Okay." She nodded.

I told her something I had just learned about the nineteen young men who had hijacked the four airliners and used them as flying bombs to kill more than three thousand innocent people. The night before, they had read a prayer-laden letter from their Al-Qaeda superiors regarding their last night on earth. The instructions written in Arabic read in part:

> *Be obedient on this night because you will be facing situations that are the ultimate and that would not be done except with full obedience.*
>
> *When you engage in battle, strike as the heroes would strike. As God says, strike above the necks and strike from everywhere. . .and then you will know all the heavens are decorated in the best way to meet you.[1]*

"These young people," I said, "had deep religious convictions, and as far as they were concerned, they were advancing a just and holy war against evil in the world. So they felt that they were right."

I could sense the wheels turning in Heather's head. I pressed on.

"So how can you say they were wrong, when they believed with all their hearts that Allah, their God, was pleased with what they did?"

Heather paused for a long moment, then said, "I guess I can't really say why it was wrong, but I know it was wrong."

I nodded and smiled. "Well, honey, you're not alone. Most people can't explain the why question either. And there's a reason for that."

I went on to explain that most Americans subscribe to a view of morality called "cultural ethics." They believe that whatever is acceptable in that culture is moral. If the majority of people say a thing is right, then it is right.

"And I can tell you," I said, "the vast majority of people in America believe the terrorists were evil and what they did was morally wrong."

Heather nodded in full agreement. "But," I continued, "there's a problem with that. Just because the majority of a group believe something doesn't make it right or wrong. For example, during World War II the citizens of Hitler's Germany believed they were morally right to launch a war against their neighbors and purge their country of whoever they felt was inferior. That led Hitler to order the murder of six million innocent Jews. So if we base our moral sense on cultural ethics, how can we say they were wrong? The majority in Hitler's country agreed with it, so it was okay, right?"

Heather's nodding changed to a slow shaking of her head.

"No, that's not right," she responded.

"In fact," I went on to say, "the Nazis offered that very argument as a defense at the Nuremberg Trials. They argued, 'How can you come from another culture and condemn what we did when we acted according to what our culture had determined to be acceptable?'"

"The Nuremberg tribunal," I continued, "was caught in a dilemma. If they applied cultural ethics to the horrors of the Holocaust, they would have had no moral grounds on which to condemn those crimes against humanity. But they didn't appeal to a cultural ethic. In condemning the Nazis, the tribunal said that there is something beyond culture and above culture that determines right and wrong."

I told Heather that they were right, of course. They recognized the need for an objective morality, but they couldn't arrive at a true moral code unless they were willing to accept a moral standard that exists beyond the individual and above culture. And that standard is God Himself.

What was I trying to do for Heather? I was attempting to lead her to see that all our laws and the principles behind them are right and true only if they are founded on and derived from the loving and perfect God of the universe. I was leading her to the person of God as the universal standard for determining right and wrong.

We err, like Brad did, when we see biblical rules and commands in isolation from God. Brad could quote a scripture passage that says lusting after a woman is wrong. That was the precept or law that he gave his son to follow. But Jayden, influenced by the postmodern culture, tends to see law as arbitrary and subjectively applied. Brad failed to break through Jayden's subjective mind-set, which he could have done by linking that precept to the person of God. He needed to understand and convey to his son that the *precepts* and *principles* of moral truths are rooted in the very *person* of God.

I asked Heather if scripture commands us not to murder. She easily knew the answer, of course, and quoted as her proof text the sixth of the Ten Commandments: "You must not murder" (Exodus 20:13). That's the precept. I asked her from what principle that precept was derived. After a bit of discussion, she stated that the precept was grounded in the biblical principle of "respecting life." She was right. All throughout scripture we find admonitions to honor and respect life and our bodies as life's physical repository. "Don't you realize that your body is the temple of the Holy Spirit, who lives in you and was given to you by God? You do not belong to yourself. . . . So you must honor God with your body" (1 Corinthians 6:19–20).

Respecting life is the principle, yet that principle finds its genesis in something else—the person of God. God is the very Spirit of life, and without Him we have no life. Scripture reports that God is the source of human life, which occurred when He formed man's body and then "breathed the breath of life into the man's nostrils, and the man became a living person" (Genesis 2:7). A little later scripture again affirms God as the author of life: "Look now," God said, "I myself am he! There is no other god but me! I am the one who kills and gives life" (Deuteronomy 32:39). Life begins and ends with God.

The prohibition against murder is a truth that is grounded in a principle much deeper than mere written law. Its validity is rooted in a source outside you and me. It is above all cultures and beyond all humanity. It is a universal truth because God and God alone is the giver and preserver of life. To arbitrarily take a life from another is to usurp God's authority as ruler over all of life. It is an offense against Him. God as the original life-giver is the supreme authority over life—only He has the right to give it and take it away.

Every law in scripture finds its origin in the person of a loving God. The precepts give us the commands, and the principles give us the "why" behind the commands. But every biblical precept that leads to a broader principle directs us ultimately to the loving person of God for the purpose of relationship. That is the reason for the precepts in the first place—to lead us to a relationship with the person of God.

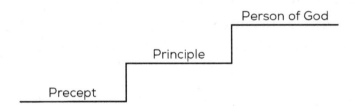

The Bible says that God spoke to Moses "face to face, as one speaks to a friend" (Exodus 33:11). Afterward Moses prayed, "If you are pleased with me, teach me your ways so I may know you" (Exodus 33:13 NIV). Moses recognized that learning God's ways—understanding His precepts and the principles behind them—would acquaint him with the person of God Himself. Ultimately God doesn't simply want our strict obedience to a set of rules and commands. As He told Hosea the prophet, "I want you to show love, not offer sacrifices. I want you to know me more than I want burnt offerings" (Hosea 6:6). This is why Jesus said, "And this is the way to have eternal life—to know you, the only true God, and Jesus Christ, the one you sent to earth" (John 17:3).

God wants to be in relationship with His creation, and His laws are designed to lead us to Him.

When we teach our kids that murder or lying or sexual immorality are wrong by pointing them to the relational God from which those prohibitions come, we do more than just lay down arbitrary rules; we teach them to know the One true God. As I mentioned above, lying and dishonesty are wrong because the righteous God is true. Justice is right because a fair God is just. Hatred is wrong because a compassionate God is love. Forgiveness is right because a tenderhearted God is mercy. Sexual immorality is wrong because a holy God is faithful and pure. These things are right or wrong, not because a culture or the church teaches them, not even because the Bible proclaims them. These things are right or wrong because they are either contrary to or consistent with the nature of a loving, relational God.

Placing scriptural instructions and rules for your kids within this relational context is critical in the process of setting them free to determine what is right and what is wrong. They need to see that behind those rules there is a compassionate God who loves and cares for them. He doesn't issue commands to restrict them, but to free them—free them to enjoy the benefits of living in God's likeness.

It is important that our kids see that right is defined within the person of God. But just as important, they must see the positive reinforcement that occurs when we do what is right. When we obey God's commands, we can count on His protection and provision. On the reverse side, negative consequences eventually occur when we fail to do the right thing.

Jayden insisted that his internet porn habits weren't hurting anyone. The truth is, all wrongdoing not only hurts God, but others as well. Most often it hurts the person engaging in the misbehavior even though he or she may not immediately realize it. In the next two chapters, we will explore how this principle works and how to share it with our young people.

CHAPTER 4

Rules for a Reason

*I*t was a typical Friday evening at the Jefferies household. Brad was dozing in his recliner, Aubrey was catching up on her emails, and Jayden was holed up as usual in his bedroom. Aubrey's phone vibrated.

"Hello."

"Mrs. Jefferies?" said the voice on the line.

"Yes, this is Aubrey Jefferies." She made her way out of the living room to avoid waking up Brad. After completing the phone call she returned to the living room with tears in her eyes.

"Brad," she said as she touched her husband's arm.

Brad started slightly at his wife's touch. "What's up?"

"We have a big problem," Aubrey began. "Teresa Karnes just called me. Her daughter Zoe has been seeing Jayden for the last couple months." She took a deep breath as she tried to maintain her composure. "Teresa said she just caught Zoe Snapchatting nude pictures of herself to our son. She said Jayden has been requesting them!"

"What?" Brad sat bolt upright in his chair. "Who's sending pictures?"

"Zoe," Aubrey answered. "Jayden's girlfriend. And Teresa claims she's been sending them for the past couple of weeks."

The two went immediately to Jayden's room. Aubrey attempted to open the door unannounced. It was locked.

"Open this door right now, young man!" she demanded.

Moments later the door opened, and Aubrey and Brad moved into Jayden's room.

"I just got a call from Zoe's mother"—Aubrey's voice quivered with anger—"and she told me you've been asking Zoe to send you nude pictures of her on your phone."

"I don't know what you're talking about," Jayden responded.

"Give me your phone, Jayden." Aubrey held out her hand. "Right now; give me your phone!"

Jayden reluctantly handed the phone to his mother. Aubrey immediately began looking for pictures, and sure enough, he had taken screenshots of the snaps. After a long moment of tense silence, she sighed, shook her head slowly, and said, "I found them."

Aubrey could no longer control her anger. "Jayden, after all we've been through with you these past few weeks, you top it off with this. Do you know how humiliating it was for me to hear that from Mrs. Karnes? I couldn't be more ashamed of you right now!"

Jayden sat down slowly on his bed, saying nothing.

Aubrey glared at Brad and said, "We're raising a pervert, and it's your fault!" Then she turned on her heel and stalked out of the room.

Brad's eyes fixed on Jayden, who was staring at the floor. "You are permanently grounded, young man!"

Shaping the Brain, for Good or Bad

The titillating photo texting between Jayden and Zoe may seem like extreme behavior, but it's not. Among teenagers today "sexting"—texting sexually explicit messages or nude images—is not uncommon at all. The Porn Phenomenon Study reveals that 62 percent of our teens and young adults have received a nude image on their electronic devices (most often through smartphones).[1]

Forty percent of our kids have sent a nude image. "Senders most often send images to their boyfriend or girlfriend (75 percent), which may indicate that sexting is becoming an acceptable practice of dating culture."[2] This type of "self-pornification" has become commonplace and can result in far-reaching ramifications.

First, distributing sexually explicit images of minors is illegal, even when the electronic distribution is by a minor. Second, when a boyfriend circulates a nude picture of his girlfriend, it can have a damaging emotional impact on the girl.

In Lacey, Washington, a fourteen-year-old girl snapped a full-length photo of herself naked and sent it by phone to a potential new boyfriend. This "Prince Charming" circulated the photo to dozens of other students. The young girl was instantly infamous in her middle school. She endured being called a "slut" and a "whore" by students who barely knew her. The boy who sent the nude image, along with his two accomplices, was eventually charged with distributing child pornography—a Class C felony. All these students were in eighth grade.[3]

Even if young people don't get caught, as did those in Lacey, Washington, sexting can have far-reaching negative ramifications. Remember in the first chapter we talked about the plasticity of the brain. Among adolescents the brain is very malleable and capable of being reshaped in response to experiences, especially repetitive experiences. When teenagers whose limbic brain system is in rapid growth view pornography on a consistent basis, it can produce highly negative results.

Neurologists have discovered a hormone called *oxytocin* that some have called the "bonding hormone." Oxytocin is a chemical the brain releases during sexual intercourse and the activity leading up to it. When this chemical is released, it prompts feelings of caring, affection, and attachment. That is one of the purposes of sex—to reinforce intimacy between a husband and a wife. However, when sexual arousal is due to a pornographic image, intimacy and attachment is misdirected.

When a person repeatedly views sexually explicit images and masturbates to them, oxytocin is released in the brain. But instead of bonding to a real person, the viewer begins bonding to a set of pixels on a screen. The more a person uses porn, the more he or she constructs imaginary intimacy with a set of fantasized images rather than with a real person as God designed.

The real problem is that repetitive pornographic experiences tend to train the brain to respond sexually only to pictures. Studies are now showing that when consistent porn users want to be sexually active with a real person, they struggle to perform sexually. In other words, their malleable brain has been so "programmed" to be sexually stimulated by pornography that when they enter the real world of human sexual relationships, their body simply doesn't cooperate. It tends to respond only to the stimulus of porn.

Major media outlets are beginning to report this phenomenon. Recently *Time* magazine ran a cover story entitled "Porn: Why Young Men Who Grew Up with Internet Porn are Becoming Advocates for Turning It Off." The article chronicles how many of today's porn users are unable to perform sexually with a real person.

> *A growing number of young men are convinced that their sexual responses have been sabotaged because their brains were virtually marinated in porn when they were adolescents. Their generation has consumed explicit content in quantities and varieties never*

before possible, on devices designed to deliver content swiftly and privately, all at an age when their brains were more plastic—more prone to permanent change—than in later life. These young men feel like unwitting guinea pigs in a largely unmonitored decade-long experiment in sexual conditioning. The results of the experiment, they claim, are literally a downer.[4]

If Jayden continues his use of internet or sexting porn, it will no doubt have a negative effect on his future marriage. In his essay "Pornography's Effects on Adults and Children," psychologist Dr. Victor Cline argues that adults who regularly masturbate to pornography risk disturbing the bonded relationship with their spouse. This practice, he writes,

Dramatically reduces their capacity to love (e.g., it results in a marked dissociation of sex from friendship, affection, caring, and other normal healthy emotions and traits which help marital relationships). In time, the "high" obtained from masturbating to pornography becomes more important than real life relationships.[5]

Research suggests that porn use undermines marital exclusivity and fidelity. "Partners feel betrayed when they discover that their partner has been viewing pornography, which is perceived as infidelity."[6] Women reported a decrease in sexual intimacy and closeness due to their spouse's porn use and "described their partner's sexual advances as conveying a message of objectification as opposed to meaningful interaction."[7]

Continued use of porn not only destroys trust and causes damage to marital relationships, it objectifies and demeans women; exploits men, women, and even children; and tears down the social fabric of morality in a culture.

The use of pornography is but one example of how disregarding the guidelines God has given us brings negative consequences. From the beginning, humans have consistently resisted these guidelines. And they have paid a price for their resistance. God provided Israel with clear laws of conduct, yet they repeatedly violated them. Scripture records that, "disaster came upon the nation of Israel because the people worshipped other gods, sinning against the Lord their God, who brought them safely out of their slavery in Egypt" (2 Kings 17:7NLT[1]). The result of disobedience is always the same: pain and suffering, heartache and ruin, destruction and death. History records it, and we see it all around us; we even experience it in our own families and churches. But God never intended for us to suffer these types of negative consequences. It was because of His love that He gave us His law and clear instructions for successful and joyful living—He wants to protect us and to provide for us.

Rules: For Our Protection and Provision

Some people react to God's laws negatively. They see His commands as constricting and biblical morality as confining. They don't see the benefits of a moral lifestyle. They fail to realize that God's commands are like those of a loving parent. "Don't touch the stove," "Look both ways before you cross the street," "Eat your vegetables," and similar commands are not meant to spoil our

---

1. Scriptures marked NLT use the NLT 1996 version.

fun and make us miserable; they are meant to protect us. God gave commands such as "Flee sexual immorality," "Husbands, love your wives," "You shall not commit adultery," and all the others because He loves us and wants to protect us and provide for us. He didn't concoct those rules just to be a killjoy or to throw His weight around; He gave them because He knows some things about health and happiness that we don't. He knows, for example, that sexual immorality is a path, not to true satisfaction and fulfillment, but to dysfunction, emptiness, and frustration. And our relational God doesn't want that for us.

Moses acknowledged this truth when he challenged the nation of Israel:

> *Now, Israel, what does the LORD your God require from you, but to fear the LORD your God, to walk in all his ways and love him, and to serve the LORD your God with all your heart and with all your soul, and to keep the LORD's commandments and His statutes which I am commanding you today for your good? (Deuteronomy 10:12–13 NASB)*

The relevance of God's laws to each of us is simply this—*they are for our good!* His laws are like the guardrails on a curvy road—they are placed there to assure safe passage. His commands are like the high fences around an electrical station—they keep us from the harm of high voltage. His instructions are like a traffic signal—they are there to smooth the traffic flow and avoid collisions. God's rules for moral behavior are motivated by love and given for our benefit. That is what we must impress upon our young people.

Brad and Aubrey were offended when Jayden lied to them

about his viewing of internet porn. In their angry response, they failed to impress on him the reason that pornography and lying are wrong. Therefore, their moral lesson had no effect. He began to view nude pictures in a different way and lied again when accused of it. The parental lesson failed because Brad and Aubrey stopped short of showing Jayden the ultimate reason for the prohibition. God made truth a moral imperative because He wanted to protect us from the consequences of lying. Brad and Aubrey could have used Jayden's offense to lead him to see this, and to appreciate the caring, loving, true God who made lying wrong for humanity's own good. By aligning with God and His standard of honesty, Jayden could be...

- protected from guilt and provided with a clear conscience and unbroken fellowship with God
- protected from shame and provided with a sense of accomplishment
- protected from the cycle of deceit and provided with a reputation of integrity
- protected from ruined relationships and provided with a trusting relationship with his parents

Jayden, and all our young people, need to know that God is not against them. He wants to see them lead happy and fulfilled lives. And living consistent with God's nature and ways provides just that. It's true that doing the right thing doesn't always result in an immediate blessing. But the blessing will come eventually. Scripture reminds us, "Even if you suffer for doing what is right, God will reward you for it" (1 Peter 3:14).

King David and his son King Solomon understood the value and rewards of God's commands when they wrote the following passages.

Joyful are people of integrity, who follow the instructions of the LORD. Joyful are those who obey his laws and search for him with all their hearts. (Psalm 119:1–2)

Make me walk along the path of your commands, for that is where my happiness is found. (Psalm 119:35)

This is how I spend my life: obeying your commandments. (Psalm 119:56)

My child, listen to what I say, and treasure my commands. Tune your ears to wisdom, and concentrate on understanding. . . . Then you will understand what is right, just, and fair, and you will find the right way to go. For wisdom will enter your heart, and knowledge will fill you with joy. Wise choices will watch over you. Understanding will keep you safe. (Proverbs 2:1–2, 9–11)

Rules without a Relationship Lead to Rebellion

Since God's rules, instructions, and guidelines are meant for our good, you'd think that when rules are imposed on our kids, they would understand and respond: "Thanks, Dad, for these rules, I really appreciate it." Or "Great, Mom! I'm so happy you've given me these guidelines." I would guess, however, that such responses are completely foreign to your ears. This is because rules don't initially feel like our friends. We love freedom, and rules, guidelines, and boundaries tend to restrict us. So it's natural to resist what feels like a limitation to our freedom.

But have you noticed that it is very rare for our children to express resentment to the actual rule that restricts them? Almost every time, their immediate reaction is not against the rule, but the rule-giver. You are the bad guy. That's why it is so important to place each rule solidly within the context of a loving and caring relationship. God places all His rules within a relational context, and we must follow suit. Unless your kids can sense your loving motivation behind every boundary you give them, their natural tendency will be to rebel and resist you *and* your guidelines.

For your kids to make right moral choices consistently, they must understand mentally and feel emotionally that the rules or instructions they are following are for their protection and provision. And they must have a strong sense that those rules are coming from someone who cares for them. The problem is that many kids don't feel that way. This is because parents and gatekeepers struggle with issuing rules squarely within the context of a compassionate and caring relationship.

I had just finished speaking to a group on parenting when a man came up and clutched my arm. "Josh, what can I do about my kids?" This father sounded desperate. He said he had three children—aged seventeen, thirteen, and ten—and then added, "They're the worst kids in my church—and I'm the pastor. I've done everything I know to do. I've drilled God's truth into them constantly. I've made them memorize scripture. They know what is expected of them; I lay down the rules very clearly. But they are rebelling, and they're ticked off at me most of the time. What can I do?"

This father was trying in every way to get his kids to do the right things. Although he didn't say it, I'm sure he wanted them to be happy and knew their misbehavior would eventually cause them pain.

I touched him on the shoulder, looked directly into his eyes, and said. "Brother, my advice to you is to back off the rules."

"What?" he responded in disbelief. "That's what's wrong—they're not obeying any rules now, and they don't even think they need to!"

"I know what you're saying," I replied, "but I repeat, lay off emphasizing the rules."[8]

The Bible has a message for dads who are trying to teach their kids right but are ticking them off instead. "Fathers, do not provoke your children to anger by the way you treat them" (Ephesians 6:4 NLT). How we as dads treat our kids can "provoke them to anger." That is what my pastor friend was doing—holding his kids to the rules but provoking them to anger in the process.

Let's look at what the Bible means when it says "provoke." Ephesians 6 translates the term from the Greek word *parorgizo*, which literally means to "arouse to wrath." The passage is telling parents not to tick their kids off by the way they deal with them. And one of the fastest ways to tick kids off is to issue rules for rules' sake. Rules that are not served up in the broth of love tend to "provoke your children to anger."

The New International Version translates this verse, "Do not *exasperate* your children." J. B. Phillips renders it, "Don't *over-correct* your children or make it difficult for them to obey the commandment." And the *Living Bible* says: "Don't keep on *scolding and nagging* your children, making them angry and resentful." The Bible also says: "Do not aggravate your children, or they will become discouraged" (Colossians 3:21 NLT). Scripture makes it clear that we parents are to treat our kids in such a way as to avoid angering them. Sure, the Bible commands children to obey their parents, but it also enjoins parents to use methods of childrearing that encourage willing obedience. How do we do this? How do we place rules within a relational context that induces a positive response and avoids a negative reaction? Let's first tackle the task of avoiding a negative reaction and in the next chapter examine how to elicit a positive response.

When it comes to issuing rules and instructions, parents and others who lead our kids tend to gravitate toward opposite ends of the spectrum. At one end we find the high-control, autocratic style of parenting that emphasizes rules over relationship. At the other end is the indifferent or permissive style that relaxes the rules but fails to focus on a healthy parent-child relationship. Both styles generate negative responses from our kids because neither places rules within the context of a loving relationship.

The Inattentive or Permissive Style

Brad is trying hard to guide his son down a good path. He wants Jayden to make right moral choices. But he is focused on his job, which dominates his time. Jayden complained that his dad wasn't around long enough to "get on the same page" with him. In other words, Brad was failing to connect relationally with his son. It takes more than just being a parent to make a kid feel loved. If parents want their children to obey them willingly, they must be actively involved in their children's lives. It's the only way their children can know that the rules are there for their benefit.

When parents distance themselves and let their kids pretty much do what they want, they are typically no happier than children in autocratic homes. Whether consciously or subconsciously, kids want boundaries. It makes them feel secure and protected. They may or may not realize it at the time, but boundaries make them feel loved. Without rules or boundaries, an unexpressed feeling is sure to lurk somewhere deep within their psyche that runs something like this: *If my parents cared about me, they'd be more interested in what I'm doing. I guess they don't really care.*

When children are parented indifferently, they become hurt and angry. That was me—the kid whose dad was always too drunk to give time to his young son. Having an absentee alcoholic father left me angry. I was angry that his drinking had brought such division to my home. I was angry that he was rarely sober. And I was angry that he had caused such pain in my mother's life. But more than anything, I felt alone.

Once I became a father, I committed to God and Dottie that I would not be an inattentive father. Although my life involved considerable travel, I was intent on *being with* my kids when I was home. I made it a point to enter their world so I could know them truly for who they were and what they were going through. I wanted them to always know that the rules were there because I loved them.

Sometimes it helps to get a little creative in finding ways of entering their world. When my son, Sean, was around ten years old, he was really into sports cars. He often cut out magazine pictures of cars like the Maserati, the Lamborghini, and the Ferrari Testarossa. He pinned them up on his bedroom wall and thought they were so cool.

I noticed his newfound interest, and one day I really surprised him. I had looked through the Yellow Pages and picked out some of the top sports car dealerships in Beverly Hills. Then I sent each car dealer a letter that said,

> *I'm a desperate dad. I'll do anything to spend time*
> *with my son, and right now he's into sports cars. If I*

pulled him out of school and brought him up to your showroom, would it be possible for us to take some test drives? I want to tell you up front, I'm not interested in buying a car.

Amazingly, I got positive replies from every dealer. I called and made appointments, and we drove up to Beverly Hills (a distance of some 150 miles) for a day in the sports car showrooms. And what a day it was! I waited in the showrooms while Sean went out on "test drives" with salesmen and "tried out" just about every big-name car you can think of. As he came by the showroom in each car, he always waved to me with an irrepressible ear-to-ear grin stretching across his face. He was so proud.

Along with the test drives, we got posters, some of which were autographed by famous race car drivers. It was an incredible day. On the way home, I asked Sean which cars he liked best and chatted about all the flyers, books, and posters he had collected. Then I gently switched the subject and started asking him how our Christian values related to spending a lot of money on expensive sports cars.

"You know, Sean," I said, "all these cars are fun, but they cost huge amounts of money. Let's think about what God has called us to value as a family." Through a series of questions, I began to probe the difference in the value of those cars and the value of God's love for us. . .what Christ did on the cross. . .what that means in terms of how we use our resources and how we fulfill the purpose of our creation. And with that beginning, I led my ten-year-old son to discover the emptiness of materialism in a way that was much more effective than simply giving him a set of rules on how to spend money wisely.

Sean never forgot that lesson on materialism and how we determine what we value in life. But I'm convinced that the lesson would have never stuck if I hadn't entered my son's world and *been with* him emotionally and relationally. Later when it came time for me to enforce some rules in Sean's life, he was assured it was because I loved him and wanted to provide for him and protect him.

The Autocratic Style

"Have you finished your homework yet?" "Did you take out the trash like I told you?" "You were supposed to be in by 10 p.m. Were you?" These are the types of questions a high-control parent would ask. It's not the line of questioning that characterizes this style; it's the attitude behind the questions—the parent's heavy-handed use of authority. The high-control parent—the *autocratic* parent—is all about the rules.

You probably sensed that Aubrey tended toward the autocratic style. She revealed this tendency in her response to Jayden after learning he had been receiving nude photos: "Do you know how humiliating it was for me to hear that from Mrs. Karnes?" This wasn't the sentiment of a grieving parent who was focused on the fallout her son might experience from his wrong actions. This was the anger of a parent who was personally humiliated because rules were broken.

Living with an autocratic parent generally causes kids to react in one of two ways: *flight* or *fight*. But in each case the response is typically accompanied by anger. When children choose flight, they may not literally run away from home, but they withdraw emotionally and relationally. They learn to go it alone and to "be obedient"—at least on the surface. Inside, however, they are probably seething.

Forced obedience at the hand of a high-control parent rarely produces a child who is motivated to do what is right, even when he or she quietly complies with the rules. A dominated child is a frustrated and angry child on the inside—one who obeys only because he is forced.

When kids choose to fight, however, their anger breaks out in the open. That was the case with my pastor friend whose kids were in open rebellion. They saw the rules clearly. They also saw how those rules were being enforced, and they didn't like it at all. Jayden was angry at the strict new rules that locked him out of his computer and grounded him permanently. But the real target of his anger and rebellion wasn't just the rules; it was against an angry mother who he felt hated him.

Aubrey clearly doesn't hate Jayden. She just wants him to stop doing wrong and start doing right. On the surface, it might seem that stricter enforcement of the rules should achieve that end. But you can be sure that strict enforcement alone will not create within a child the inner motivation to make right choices on his own. Our objective must be something much higher than simply getting a child to comply with the rules.

What is it that you really want from your kids? You want them to love you. You want them to understand that the rules are there to protect them and provide for them. You want them to be motivated to make right choices. There is a key to accomplish those things, and in the next chapter we'll see that Jesus Himself demonstrates how to use it.

CHAPTER 5

The Empowering Nature of Grace

It was late. The kids were in bed, and Brad and Aubrey were sitting alone at the kitchen table. Brad stared down at his tea as he absently stirred it, wanting to say something but struggling with how to begin. Finally, he cleared his throat and said, "Honey, I know this. . .this problem with Jayden, coming on top of. . .of what we've been through over the last three months has been difficult for you." He looked up at his wife. She was gazing off into the living room.

"I know you've forgiven me," Brad continued, "but I also know it still plagues you. I was so wrong, and I dearly hope that in time trust between us can be fully restored. And now with Jayden, it's got to have made it all even worse."

Aubrey continued to stare into the living room as if Brad had not spoken. He reached over and touched her hand gently. "I'm so sorry, honey," he said softly. Aubrey did not move, but Brad could see tears glistening in her eyes.

Finally, she spoke. "I know, Brad. You've been good these past months, making yourself accountable and all." She paused, trying to hold back the tears. "And I'm sorry, too. I shouldn't have blamed you for Jayden's problem. It's just that. . ." She could hold it no longer. Her tears overflowed, and she began to weep openly.

Brad scooted his chair toward her and enfolded her in his arms. She buried her head in his shoulder and sobbed. After the tears subsided, she slowly lifted her head.

"Brad," she began, "I don't want Jayden to feel that I'm ashamed of him. But I know he does after all I've said and the way I've responded to what he did. I really love our son, and I want him to know I'm here to help him." Aubrey again laid her head onto Brad's shoulder.

"I know you do, dear," he said softly as he stroked his wife's head. "I do too. We've just got to find a way to let him know we love him regardless of what he's done."

"What if we tell him he's no longer grounded," Audrey whispered.

"That would really shock him, wouldn't it?"

The Barrier of Shame

Here within the Jeffries family we have a household filled with shame. First, Brad, as you may have guessed, is filled with shame for betraying his wife with his own indulgence in internet pornography, even though it was short lived.

Brad is not a rare case. The Porn Phenomenon Study revealed that 87 percent of men ages 31–50 periodically come across internet porn and 63 percent actively seek it out.[1] Christian men are not exempt from this struggle. Studies show the same percentage of Christian men regularly view internet pornography.[2] Not only do Christian laypeople deal with this struggle; it affects church leaders as well. The Porn Phenomenon Study found that 64 percent of youth pastors and 57 percent of senior pastors admitted to presently or previously struggling with the use of internet porn.[3]

Dr. Ted Roberts is the founder and Clinical Director of Pure Desires Ministries of Gresham, Oregon. He and his ministry have treated hundreds of Christian laypeople and ministers who are struggling with porn addiction. Dr. Roberts states:

We've done clinical studies in 3,000 data points in evangelical churches. These are not self reported; these are clinical evaluations. We've discovered that 60-72% of men in the church are sex addicts. 50-58% of pastors are sex addicts. 24-30% of women are sex addicts.[4]

Internet porn use among Christians and within the church seems to be an unspoken problem. Many would like help in overcoming their addiction, but few know where to turn. Of those adults caught in the grip of internet porn and wanting to stop, 87 percent say that no one in their lives is helping them avoid pornography. And 54 percent of those couldn't even think of anyone who could help them.[5] The lack of help and support for those struggling with this problem is revealed in the fact that only 7 percent of churches in the United States have a program specifically designed to help people who are struggling with porn use.[6]

The widespread use of pornography is abetted by its secretive nature. It is a hidden sin that feeds on its secrecy. The greatest fear of most pornography users, especially Christians, is the fear of exposure. That fear is intensified to a paralyzing level by the feeling of shame.

Brad felt guilty for viewing internet porn in secret. He knew he shouldn't be viewing it, but its allure, combined with its secretive nature, compelled him to take the risk. When this was finally exposed to Aubrey, he felt extreme shame. Guilt told him, "I did something bad." Shame told him, "I am bad."

An unhealthy shame, that Brad and so many feel when they've done wrong, is what Christian Therapist and Pastoral Coach Jayson Graves calls "toxic shame." He says, "Toxic shame is a chronic or lasting negative feeling or thought about our identity. Guilt, on the other hand, is a negative feeling about our behavior."[7] This unhealthy shame tells us we're flawed and unworthy of love. It breeds negative feelings about our identity—who we believe we are as a person. Brad, like so many, attached his self-worth to his actions. So rather than simply feeling guilty for the bad thing he had done, he felt that he was a bad person. And this wasn't isolated to just him. Aubrey, like most wives of internet porn sex addicts, experienced this toxic shame as well.

A spouse is not at fault for her partner's indiscretions, but she often feels she doesn't measure up to the virtual women with whom her husband is having an "affair." She feels she's not good enough to satisfy her husband. As a result, self-esteem takes a nosedive. The spouse tends to feel worthless and inadequate.

When pornography use enters a marriage, the most sacred element of the marital relationship—trust—is shattered. The wife can no longer trust the man who vowed "to love and to cherish" her no matter what. He has violated that trust, and it will require a painstaking and intentional process to rebuild it.

In our story, Brad felt a toxic shame. Aubrey felt this kind of shame. And Jayden felt it as well. We have explained why Brad and Aubrey felt shame, but why would Jayden feel this after excusing his porn use as "no big deal" and "not wrong for him"? There are two reasons: First, he subconsciously knew that porn is wrong. Throughout his life, his parents, preachers' sermons, and Sunday school classes had all condemned porn, and even the culture's postmodern influences could not completely override that embedded teaching.

Second, even though Jayden may have convinced himself that porn use is "no big deal," he still valued the affirmation of his parents. They thought porn was wrong, so he did not want his porn use exposed to their negative judgment. He, like his entire generation, equated what he did with who he was, and he felt that his parents would apply that standard in their relationship to him. In other words, if they found that he was using porn, not only would they judge what he did as bad; they would judge him personally as bad. Until parents and gatekeepers of youth help kids overcome that fallacy, it will be nearly impossible for them to feel truly loved.

Brad and Aubrey love their son dearly, but Jayden finds it hard to feel that love. If you asked him why, he'd probably say, "My parents think I am a bad person because I like porn." What he should think—and what his parents would like him to think—is something more like, "My parents love me, but they don't like what I've been doing." This misunderstanding is perhaps the most common barrier to positive parent-child relationships today. It explains why the misbehavior of kids prevents them from feeling assurance of their parents' love. Even when parents place the rules within the context of loving relationships, that love often fails to penetrate their children's barrier of shame. Our kids feel that the bad they have done defines who they are, and that erroneous assumption produces shame. Consequently, they can't receive love because they don't feel worthy of it.

The same holds true for adults who have fallen prey to internet pornography, especially ministers. The Porn Phenomenon Study shows that 94 percent of youth pastors and 87 percent of pastors who use porn feel shame about it.[8] Yet they aren't about to share their failure with the elders of the church or their congregation. Only 8 percent of these pastors indicated that their elders knew of their struggle, and virtually no one within the congregation was aware of their problem.[9]

One of the primary reasons pastors don't confess their struggle is the fear that their elders and congregation will react with rejection. The Study confirms the validity of that fear. Seventy percent of Christians say a pastor should leave the ministry if he uses porn.[10] That kind of rejection does nothing but fuel shame.

Unless we help those we love deal with the unhealthy shame they carry, they will not be convinced that they are worthy of our love. Rules and discipline are not a cure for shame. That doesn't mean rules and discipline aren't necessary; it simply means that they aren't the tools one needs to get at the heart of the problem. What Jayden needs and what we all need, first and foremost, is to be set free to experientially know that we are loved for who we are regardless of what we've done. And that freeing agent is grace. It is grace that can penetrate our soul, dispel toxic shame, and set us free to know that we are loved for who we are.

Our Model of Grace

Do you tend to believe that what you do defines who you are? When you fail to accomplish a goal, do you tend to feel that you are a failure? When you do something bad, does it make you feel that you are a bad person? Many people today have fallen for the concept that we are what we do. If it were written out as an equation, it would look like this:

Who I Am = What I Do

Based on that thinking, who you are is inseparable from what you do and think and believe. Your entire identity is wrapped up in your performance. Since Brad and his son have adopted this perspective, it stands to reason that they are going to continue to live a life of shame for viewing internet pornography. In their minds, their bad behavior has made them a bad person, and nothing can erase that perception. Their unhealthy shame does nothing but drive them into hiding where their addiction can fester and grow in isolation. What they need is to be shocked out of their darkness of shame and into the light of grace!

Grace is love without conditions. Grace accepts a person on the basis of *being*, rather than *doing*. You can't earn grace; it is unmerited favor. Grace looks beyond what a person does, sees what that person is, and loves what it sees. Grace accepts, forgives, and restores. And this kind of grace is personified and modeled perfectly by a particular person. If grace had a name, it would be Jesus.

Scripture tells us that "The Word [Jesus] became flesh and made his dwelling among us. We have seen his glory, the glory of the one and only Son, who came from the Father, full of grace and truth" (John 1:14 NIV). Jesus spoke the truth and laid out the laws and rules that we are to obey. But what shocked people who failed to measure up to those laws and rules was His grace-filled love. He looked beyond their behavior and saw them for who they really were—lost people who needed a friend and a Savior. He placed the rules within the loving context of grace. Rather than shaming with condemnation, he smothered people with grace. Parents, gatekeepers, and our kids need to experience that kind of Jesus every day. As unworthy as we may be, when with grateful hearts we receive His grace, it dispels the shame in our lives. That's what Jesus does—He loves, extends grace, forgives sin because of His sacrificial death, and dispels shame.

Jesus once met a man named Zacchaeus. Although he was a Jew, his fellow Jews held him in utter contempt because he was a tax collector for the despised Roman government. These outcasts not only collected Roman taxes, they added a "surcharge" on top of it, from which they profited handsomely. The Jews considered tax collectors to be deceitful traitors and thieves. It's likely that Zacchaeus's dishonorable profession had hardened him on the outside, but we cannot doubt that living day by day with the obvious contempt of his fellow countrymen caused deep inner shame.

Then along came Jesus. Zacchaeus had heard He was coming and had climbed a tree to get a better view of Him. When Jesus walked under that tree, He looked up and said something that shocked the tax collector to the core. Rather than confronting Zacchaeus as a cheating thief and traitor to his people, Jesus said, "Quick, come down! I must be a guest in your home today" (Luke 19:5). Why was this so shocking? Because in the culture of that time, good Jews would never have any kind of fellowship with such tax-collecting "scum." To have dinner with such a man was tantamount to condoning his abhorrent practices. Yet Jesus invited himself to dinner with this lying, cheating thief. That was grace in action!

How did the people respond? They were confused and distraught. "'He has gone to be a guest of a notorious sinner,' they grumbled" (Luke 19:7). The Jewish religious leaders were outraged. Jesus seemed to be disregarding this man's despicable behavior. It appeared that He wasn't reinforcing the rules or requiring strict obedience to the law. How can you correct people's bad behavior without pointing out their failure to adhere to the rules?

It's the same question facing Brad and Aubrey. How can they lead their son down a path of sexual purity without requiring adherence to biblical truth about sexuality? Jesus' approach seemed to focus more on accepting people in both their badness and goodness rather than stressing the need for such strict performance of the law. We can see why the Jews found this disturbing. Grace may eradicate toxic shame by making bad people feel completely accepted for who they are, but does that do anything to change bad behavior? The answer—which we will explore shortly—surprises most people. But first, let's reinforce the principle by looking at two more examples.

Levi, another tax collector, hosted a banquet with Jesus as the guest of honor. Shocked yet again by another of Jesus' social faux pas, the "Pharisees and their teachers of religious law complained bitterly to Jesus' disciples, 'Why do you eat and drink with such scum?'" (Luke 5:30). It makes no sense. Why would you put your welcoming arms around rule-breakers? Doesn't it just encourage more rule breaking? Jesus' action does nothing but promote more misbehavior, right?

It gets even "worse." On another occasion, a Pharisee invited Jesus over for dinner. A prostitute crashed the party and began washing Jesus' feet with perfume mixed with her tears. The offended Pharisee "said to himself, 'If this man were a prophet, he would know what kind of woman is touching him. She's a sinner'" (Luke 7:39).

What did Jesus do next? He said to the prostitute, "Your sins are forgiven" (Luke 7:48). Now, wait a minute. It's bad enough that Jesus even let this woman touch Him. An upright Jewish man would never let an immoral woman touch him in public. But to make matters worse, He forgives her! Who does He think He is? "The men at the table said among themselves, 'Who is this man, that he goes around forgiving sins?'" (Luke 7:49).

What shocked these religious leaders so much is the fact that these people were habitual sinners. We're talking about morally depraved individuals—people who had committed treachery, robbery, and sexual depravity. How can Jesus embrace these "scumbags" so openly and then apparently overlook their sin? Isn't that just going to make matters worse? If Brad and Aubrey accept Jayden without addressing his improper behavior, he'll never learn how to make right moral choices. How can such a permissive approach possibly work?

The truth is, Jesus wasn't being permissive; He was being loving. By extending grace to such obvious sinners, He did something utterly unique, and it shocked those around Him. The essence of what Jesus did was to separate who the person was from what he or she did. He separated the person from the behavior. He didn't accept the behavior; He accepted the person. Sure, Zacchaeus was a traitor and a thief; Jesus knew that. But He looked past the behavior and saw a man who felt rejected by his own people, guilty of wrongdoing, fearful, alone, and burdened with shame. Zacchaeus was a person who sinned, but he was also a lost sheep—a wayward child without a friend or a Savior.

Love wrapped in grace accepts a person for who he or she is. When grace separates the person from the performance, it drives out shame. The vocabulary of grace is, "In spite of your sins, I see you for who you really are, and I love what I see."

That's what Jayden needed to hear. He needed a grace-filled parent who could say, "I love you, Jayden, for who you are. You are my son, and you'll never do anything that will change my deep love for you." With this approach, Jayden would feel loved and be set free of shame. Shame is cast out of a life smothered by grace. Grace tells a person that he or she is worthy of love, and that love is based not on performance, but on a relationship. Shame devalues; grace affirms and builds value.

Grace does not endorse bad behavior; to the contrary, it sets a person free to make right choices. When Jesus extended grace to Zacchaeus, He didn't have to preach a sermon on honesty. As a Jew, this tax collector knew all about the Ten Commandments and the need to be honest. What was so shocking about grace was that it did what condemnation could never do: it motivated and empowered this dishonest man to change.

Jesus was probably the first respectable Jew who had ever sat at Zacchaeus's table. The man had never felt such love and acceptance, and that alone brought about a dramatic change in his life. While the dinner was in full swing, we read that "Zacchaeus stood before the Lord and said, 'I will give half my wealth to the poor, Lord, and if I have cheated people on their taxes, I will give them back four times as much!' Jesus responded, 'Salvation has come to this home today, for this man has shown himself to be a true son of Abraham. For the Son of Man came to seek and save those who are lost'" (Luke 19:8–10).

Jesus' grace has power! He brings things out of the darkness and into the light. Jesus looked beyond this man's sin and saw his need for an accepting love. Instead of feeling loathed, Zacchaeus felt loved. Instead of being condemned, he received compassion. In the presence of everyone, Jesus embraced him as a lost son and became his Savior. Through the power of grace, Zacchaeus became a changed man.

What about the prostitute? Jesus knew that the woman anointing his feet with perfume had committed prostitution, but he didn't see her first and foremost as a prostitute. He saw her as a lost child in need of acceptance and forgiveness. He "said to the woman, 'Your faith has saved you, go in peace'" (Luke 7:50).

Jesus' grace-filled love made a distinction between the *essence* and the *nature* of this woman. Her essence was a masterpiece of creation lovingly formed in the image of God. Her nature was a fallen one, being infected by a life of prostitution. He accepted her as His lost child and forgave her offenses. That's what grace-filled love does; it accepts people for who they are and forgives them for what they've done. The power of grace separates the sin from the person.

The Bible says that "your iniquities have separated you from your God" (Isaiah 59:2 NIV). Isaiah makes a clear distinction between who you are and what you do. Who you are is God's lost child, yet created in His image. What you do is sin. If what you do was the same as who you are, God couldn't remove "our sins as far from us as the east is from the west" (Psalm 103:12). God's grace-filled love has the power to accept you regardless of what you have or haven't done. His acceptance comes with no conditions attached.

Just as you can do nothing bad enough to keep God from loving you, you can do nothing good enough to earn his acceptance and forgiveness. Performance has nothing to do with it. "God showed his great love [a grace-filled love] for us by sending Christ to die for us while we were still sinners" (Romans 5:8). "God saved you by his grace when you believed. And you can't take credit for this; it is a gift from God. Salvation is not a reward for the good things we have done, so none of us can boast about it" (Ephesians 2:8–9).

It is critical to note, however, that while Jesus' grace-filled love accepts *you* without any condition, He still cannot accept *your sin*. Your sin, and everyone else's, is an enormous problem for Him. He can't overlook it; He must obliterate it, blot it out, and cancel any record of the charges against us. The deceitful tax collectors were guilty of extortion. That's the charge against them, and it can't be overlooked. The prostitute committed adultery, and her immorality can't be simply dismissed. For justice to be served, someone must pay. Forgiveness comes at a high cost, and Jesus paid that high cost with His very life.

"When we were utterly helpless, Christ came at just the right time and died for us sinners" (Romans 5:6). "God made you alive with Christ, for he forgave all our sins. He canceled the record of the charges against us and took it away by nailing it to the cross" (Colossians 2:13–14). God says, "I—yes, I alone—will blot out your sins for my sake and will never think of them again" (Isaiah 43:25).

God accepts us without condition because of who we are— His children, created in His image. Sin has made us His lost children, yet He can forgive us because of the sacrificial death and resurrection of His Son. Jesus' grace-filled love accepts us for who we are and forgives us because of His atoning sacrifice. The apostle Paul tells us to pass on this gift of grace-filled love when he says to "accept each other just as Christ has accepted you" (Romans 15:7). He goes on to say, "Let your conversation be always full of grace" (Colossians 4:6 NIV).

A Grace-Filled Style of Parenting

It is this grace-filled love that empowers us to accept our kids for who they are and forgive them for what they've done. Our acceptance removes their shame, and our forgiveness removes their guilt, and that frees our kids up to choose right. To accomplish this, we must see our young people in a new way. We must no longer equate their performance with their identity as a person. Brad and Aubrey will need to see Jayden's actions as being separate from his personhood. They must see him as their dear son whom they love, and they must recognize his wrong actions as behaviors that will bring him suffering. The *essence* of Jayden is a young man created in God's image and brought into the world by two loving parents. The *nature* of Jayden has been drawn into porn that will damage his brain, distort his view of women and God's gift of sex, and create havoc in any future relationship with a young woman.

Instead of condemning Jayden, his parents need to embrace him for who he is, their son, and feel pain for what his wrong choice will bring him. What he is doing is clearly wrong. There is no excuse for his behavior. But what Jayden needs to feel is the heartfelt pain and concern from Brad and Aubrey over the negative consequences he will face because of his misdeeds. He needs to recognize that he has acted outside of God's protection and provision, while at the same time realize that his parents are saddened because his choices are going to bring him suffering.

That is what grace-filled parenting does; it focuses on the child's well-being. When your kids sense that your ultimate concern is about their well-being, they sense you care. When your spouse senses that you have his or her interests, security, happiness, and welfare at heart, the depth of your love and care will not be in doubt.

The apostle Paul made this very point when he wrote that husbands are to "love your wives, just as Christ loved the church. He gave up his life for her. . . In the same way, husbands ought to love their wives as they love their own bodies. For a man who loves his wife actually shows love for himself. No one hates his own body but feeds and cares for it, just as Christ cares for the church" (Ephesians 5:25, 28–29).

"Each of you," Paul writes in another letter, "should look out not only to your own interests, but also to the interests of others" (Philippians 2:4 NIV). That is what grace-filled love causes a person to do. It looks out for the interest of others because it wants to protect and provide for the one it loves. This kind of love feeds, nourishes, provides, and protects. Drawing from these and other verses, we can define what grace-filled love really means. Grace-filled love means *making the security, happiness, and welfare of the other person as important as your own.*

Love wrapped in grace empowers your kids to look at rules in a fresh and positive way. As we know, most kids don't naturally consider the rules they are given to be in their best interest. They generally see rules as restrictions on their freedom. But as they experience rules within the context of a loving relationship that proves to be in their best interest, they are set free to respond positively. Scripture teaches this, and modern neuroscience confirms it.

About three thousand years ago, King Solomon wrote, "Train up a child in the way he should go, even when he is old he will not depart from it" (Proverbs 22:6 NASB). Today neurological studies confirm the validity of this scriptural admonition and promise. The way we "train up" our kids can, in a real sense, set their brains free to respond positively to our grace-filled love. When this occurs, that training will be permanently locked in.

In the previous chapter, we talked about how the brain of young people is in a plastic stage, and how it is shaped negatively by continued use of internet pornography. It is good to know that this grim phenomenon can be countered. Even if negative programming of the brain has occurred, it can be reprogrammed positively by relational experiences.

At a child's birth, every neuron in the cerebral cortex has an estimated 2,500 connections called synapses. By the age of three, this number has grown to a whopping 15,000 synapses per neuron. The average adult, however, has only about half that number.[11] The reason adults have less neuron connections is because throughout childhood, synapses that are not used and nourished are pruned. And here's the good news: The synapses that are reinforced through relational experiences survive the pruning process and remain intact. In other words, if an emerging teenager is nurtured with an array of positive physical, emotional, and relational experiences, that child's brain will develop accordingly. While a young person like Jayden may be shaping his brain in a damaging fashion through viewing internet porn, that programming can be reversed with a grace-filled style of parenting.

This style of parenting sees a child's best interest as the highest priority. It isn't so much a balancing act that tries to measure out just the right number of rules and relationships to keep things stable. It is much simpler than that. It involves placing rules within the context of a loving relationship with one's kids. The kids soon learn that rules come out of a heart of love, and their purpose is to protect them from harm and provide for their well-being. That process will shape and mold the brain in such a way that it will be "fixed" in adulthood. As wise old Solomon said, "Even when he is old he will not depart from it" (v. 6).

When young people violate the rules, grace-filled parents can reinforce in their mind that their offense is separate from their personhood. Remember that grace prompts us to say, "I love you for who you are—you are my son, my daughter. And I hate what you did because it can bring you suffering and heartache. Let's be sure you understand how to avoid this so you won't suffer on a long-term basis. I want you to know that your security, happiness, and welfare are as important to me as my own."

God designed us to follow His rules *because* of the loving relationship He has with us. There are inevitable dos and don'ts in life, and there always will be. But they are placed there to provide for our well-being and to protect us from harm. That's what a grace-filled style of parenting does; it places rules within a relationship committed to protect their children and provide for their best.

Responsible To, But Not For

You cannot, nor should you, always shield your kids from the natural consequences of their wrong choices. Sometimes our kids' misbehavior provides an opportunity to reinforce how wrong choices bring consequences.

I remember an incident that brought negative consequences to my son Sean when he was in the fifth grade. It gave Dottie and me an opportunity to affirm that we love him for who he is while at the same time allowing the consequences of his wrong choice to impact his life in a positive way.

Sean was at school when the teacher bawled out two boys for disrupting the class. The two troublemakers were Sean's soccer teammates. They were tough-guy types who held themselves aloof and hardly gave him the time of day. Sean wanted to impress these tough guys and perhaps even work his way into their favor. He decided to let them know he was on their side, and he thought a show of defiance toward the teacher would do the trick. So when she turned around to write something on the board, Sean gave her a one-finger salute.

Well, that got him noticed. Right after class, all the kids, including his two teammates, gathered around him and treated him like a celebrity. The problem was, word of his little antic got back to Dottie and me.

I admit that the incident embarrassed me a little. I could have come down hard on Sean with an "I have a reputation to protect and an image to uphold" attitude. If I had done this, I would have fallen into the self-centered trap of thinking my kid's behavior was really about me. And that would lead me to feel responsible *for* Sean's actions. But the truth is, I wasn't responsible for anything he did or didn't do. None of us parents or gatekeepers are responsible for what our kids do. Now, that may sound foreign to you. Many parents feel that they *are* responsible for their kids' actions. They feel that what their kids do, good or bad, reflects on their own parenting performance. And in one way it does. Our kids do bear our last name, and people do tend to either blame or credit parents for how their kids behave. The truth is, however, that each person makes his own individual choices, and he alone is responsible for how those choices play out.

"Pay careful attention to your own work," the apostle Paul said, "for then you will get the satisfaction of a job well done, and you won't need to compare yourself to anyone else. For we are each responsible for our own conduct" (Galatians 6:4–5). People make choices, and kids are people too. We are not responsible for other people's choices—not even those of our children.

Even the almighty God is not responsible for human behavior. He allows each of us to choose for ourselves whether we do right or wrong. We also must choose whether to have a loving relationship with Him. He gave this choice to Adam and Eve from the very beginning. That first God-and-human relationship was based on an authentic love that was to be chosen, maintained, and expressed freely and voluntarily.

In giving the first couple the freedom to choose, God took a risk. The risk was that they could choose to reject God's rule, even though it was given within the context of a loving relationship. Authentic love could not be forced; they had to choose to love Him back. It is the same today. We are free to choose God and His ways, yet He will not force us to make that choice. Our freedom to choose makes it clear that God is not responsible for the choices we make. By the same token, neither are we responsible *for* the choices our kids make. But we are to be responsible *to* our kids. We bear the responsibility to love and accept them for who they are, to teach them, to discipline them, to make ourselves available to them, to support them, to encourage, appreciate, comfort, and even to hold them accountable for their actions.

On this particular day, I felt responsible to hold Sean accountable for his actions. My son's behavior in the classroom was wrong, and he needed to be held accountable for what he had done. If Dottie and I felt responsible *for* what Sean did, we would have devised a punishment that deterred him from embarrassing us like that again. But because we felt responsible *to* Sean, we took a different path—a path of grace and accountability.

Sean, now married with three children, shares the aftermath of that incident.

> *My parents didn't ground me, deny me a meal or two, or make me go to my room. They sat me down and calmly probed to figure out what I did and why I did it. They asked me question after question that led me to*

see how disrespectful my actions were to my teacher.

I saw how I had made a wrong choice. So acknowledging my wrong wasn't such a big deal. But what they said I needed to do was. They told me I needed to apologize to my teacher in front of the entire class and also apologize to the class. My dad told me he would go with me if I wanted him to. I said I could do it on my own. It was a humbling experience. But I learned I was responsible for my actions, and actions have consequences.

Sean learned a lot through that experience. At the top of the list was the assurance that his Mom and Dad accepted him for who he was—our loved son. What he did was shameful, but he didn't need to live a life of toxic shame. His behavior was vulgar, but that one act didn't make him a vulgar person. We guided Sean to separate what he did from who he was. He felt loved for being our son and was made to feel accountable for his wrong choice. Sean was set free from his sense of shame as he received our acceptance, sought forgiveness, and apologized for his behavior.

It was during this time in our parenting that Dottie and I began to discover a process for helping our kids make right moral choices. We eventually called it the 4 C's process. None of us automatically make right choices in life. In fact, we're naturally prone to make wrong choices based on our selfish, fallen nature. Making right moral choices requires conscious and deliberate action. That is where the 4 C's process can become helpful in guiding your young people. In the remaining chapters, we will systematically walk through that process and show how to implement it in a grace-filled parenting style.

CHAPTER 6

Being Models of Right and Wrong Choices

Hey, buddy," Brad knocked on Jayden's bedroom door and called out to his son, "You there?"

"Sure, come in," came the reply.

Brad stepped into the room and said, "Grab your jacket and come take a ride with me."

"Where you going?"

"I just want you to come with me, okay?"

Reluctantly, Jayden dragged himself to the car, and the two headed down the street.

"I just want to talk with you without any interruptions," Brad began. "It's about the internet stuff."

"Awww, come on, Dad," Jayden groaned. "You guys grounded me forever, and I can't even use the computer without going through Mom. What more do you want?"

"Don't worry, Son, this isn't another lecture or anything like that. I want to tell you something about me, and I need your help."

"Help for what?"

Brad took a deep breath and glanced over to Jayden. "I told you before that a lot of guys struggle with internet porn, and I've admitted to you that I've even seen some of it when I was a kid."

"Okay," Jayden replied, drawing the word out. Where was his dad going with this?

"What I'm about to share with you is very confidential and

private. It's just between us—man to man. Okay?"

"Sure, Dad."

"I'm not proud of what I'm about to tell you, but I've done more than just see a little porn when I was young." Brad paused. It was difficult to get his words out. He continued, "Then about six months ago I began to visit a few porn sites every once in awhile."

Jayden looked straight ahead and said nothing. Brad went on.

"A little over three months ago, I confessed this to your mom. Even though I wasn't hooked on the stuff, it hurt her deeply. And I asked her to hold me accountable. Does that make sense?"

"Yeah, Dad, I think so."

"So, Son, I need your help. I'd like to ask you to be my secondary accountability partner."

"Your what?"

"My secondary accountability partner. I've signed up with a group that has targeted all my electronic devices. They track every site I visit, including YouTube videos, and they identify the search terms I use. They flag anything that's questionable and create a report listing what I see and do online. I just don't want to get addicted to porn. So your mom is my primary accountability partner. She gets every report of my internet activity so we can go over it and talk about it. But I'd like to have them send my report to you too. That way you can monitor my activity on the web along with Mom and talk to me about what I've been viewing, if it's anything problematic. What do you think; will you help me like that?"

"That's pretty heavy stuff," Jayden replied. "It would be sorta weird for me to be checking up on you. I mean, you're my dad."

"Yeah, I'm your dad. But growing older and more mature does not eliminate the struggle to make right choices. Other people who struggle with this have found that one of the best weapons against it is making yourself accountable to the people who love you. And it really does help."

"Really?" Jayden struggled to comprehend what he was hearing.

"Yeah, really. So will you be my accountability partner on this?" Brad pressed.

"Yeah, I guess so," Jayden responded. "But could you do the same with me? Could you get a report on how I use the internet so I don't have to go through Mom all the time to let me on the web?"

"Of course I will, Son. We can do this thing together."

"Yeah," Jayden said nodding. "That would be cool. We'd be helping each other out."

"By the way, you're not grounded anymore."

"I'm not?" Jayden brightened as if struck by a beam of sunlight.

"Not anymore."

"That's awesome, Dad!"

Who's Accountable to Whom?

Some readers might respond to the above story in this way:

"What is Brad doing by confessing his failure to his son and asking for help? In a sense, he is letting his child correct him, which will do nothing but encourage Jayden to disrespect his father. Telling his son that he too struggles with internet porn puts the father on the same level with his son. By asking his son to be his accountability partner he is foolishly putting himself under the authority of his son. This approach is upside down. A parent must always maintain the position of authority as the leader in the parent-child relationship."

Some parents subscribe to this view and act accordingly. But I'm convinced there is a better way. Rather than trying to earn respect from my kids by hiding my failures and pretending perfection, I prefer to earn it by demonstrating that they are highly respected themselves and have insights that can teach me. As a parent, I am a teacher, but I must never forget that I must always be a student. I have much to learn about developing a deepened relationship with my children, and they are in a unique position to help me learn.

Balancing the teacher/student role can be tricky, and being vulnerable enough to make yourself accountable to your kids can be scary. And caution must be taken if parents are thinking about revealing an internet porn struggle with a young person. It may or may not be the thing to do based on a number of varying circumstances. Get wise counsel before taking a step like that of Brad in our story. But I am convinced that mutual interchange and accountability springs from a valid philosophy and theology of leadership. In fact, it's generally a misguided view of leadership that gets us parents in trouble.

Jesus had something to say about what real leadership is all about. When you apply His teaching to parenting, you will see the wisdom of being vulnerable to your young people. Note what the Master Teacher said:

> In this world the kings and great men lord it over
> their people, yet they are called "friends of the people."
> But among you it will be different. Those who are
> the greatest among you should take the lowest rank,
> and the leader should be like a servant. Who is more
> important, the one who sits at the table or the one who

serves? The one who sits at the table, of course. But not here! For I am among you as one who serves. (Luke 22:25–27)

Here Jesus presented to His disciples a whole new concept of authority and leadership. The common view was that people were to submit to and serve leaders in authority. But Jesus turned that principle on its head; leaders are the ones who should serve. He demonstrated this revolutionary concept during the Passover meal on the night before He went to the cross. John tells us that He got up from the meal and began to wash the disciples' feet just as a servant would do. When He finished the menial task, He said, "Do you understand what I was doing? You call me 'Teacher' and 'Lord,' and you are right, because that's what I am. And since I, your Lord and Teacher, have washed your feet, you ought to wash each other's feet. I have given you an example to follow. Do as I have done to you" (John 13:12–15).

How should we apply these passages to parenting? How should parents exercise authority with their children? If we are to live out Jesus' instructions on leadership, then we are to serve the needs of our children. This inverted concept of authority is difficult for many parents to grasp. It turns the idea of leading on its ear. How do you effectively lead by serving? How do you maintain your authority by taking the lowest rank? This approach gets confusing if you try to implement it as a hierarchical structure of a teacher maintaining consistent authority over the student he instructs. But it makes sense as a relational philosophy designed to develop an intimate relationship with your kids and spouse.

As a parent, you ultimately want a relationship with your kids in which they understand that your guidance comes out of a heart of love. You want them to be responsive to your instructions and be accountable for their behavior. What better way to teach them accountability than to openly model your accountability to God and in turn make yourself accountable to them?

That may seem strange and unorthodox to some, but I believe there's no better way to gain your kids' trust, respect, and admiration than to ask them to hold you accountable.

When I began to put this model into practice myself, I started first with Dottie. I said to her, "Honey, I need your help. Will you hold me accountable as a husband and a father? If I'm on the road too much, tell me. If I'm not meeting your needs or the children's needs, spell it out for me. If I'm not spending enough time with the children or with you, I want to know about it."

"Okay, Josh," Dottie replied, a little reluctantly. "I'll tell you, but sometimes it may hurt a little."

She was right; it wouldn't be fun to hear about areas of my life in which I was failing. Yet I needed to hear the truth.

Dottie was my first step toward accountability, but I wasn't through. When Kelly's seventh birthday rolled around, I wrote a special note in her birthday card:

> *Dear Kelly, I sure love you. I count it such a joy to be*
> *your dad, but you know, I'm going to need your help*
> *this year. I've never been the father of a seven-year-old*
> *daughter before. I just want to be the best dad I can be*
> *to you. And if you ever feel that I'm not doing right or*
> *not being fair, or loving and considerate, please tell me.*

When Sean turned seven, I did the same thing with him. In fact, I've done it with all four of the children. My efforts toward family accountability have paid off in spades; my wife and kids have become my best counselors.

Sometimes their critiques stung, and I got defensive. Each time I became defensive, however, it only caused them to clam up—and I lost a great source of insight and help. This taught me a highly valued lesson: although there were moments when I had to swallow my pride in such big chunks it almost choked me, I forced myself to digest the bitter meal because I knew I couldn't get along without their help.

When we as parents and gatekeepers become vulnerable and real and admit that we struggle too, we become a powerful model to our kids. We don't need to be perfect models, just authentic models. The apostle Paul understood being authentic. He told the Christians in Corinth that he'd had many spiritual experiences he could boast about. But he said, "I won't do it. I don't want anyone to think more highly of me than what they can actually see in my life and my message" (2 Corinthians 12:6 NLT).

In using his own life as a model for others to follow, Paul was not lowering the standard of Christlike living. In fact, he told the Corinthians, "Follow my example, as I follow the example of Christ" (1 Corinthians 11:1 NIV). His goal was to be an authentic model of Christlikeness. This didn't mean he should put on a mask or try to position himself as a perfect leader. It meant being authentic and not hiding the fact that he had weaknesses. He admitted:

> I don't mean to say that I have already achieved these
> things or that I have already reached perfection! But
> I keep working toward the day when I will finally be
> all that Christ Jesus saved me for and wants me to be.
> (Philippians 3:12 NLT)

On another occasion Paul said:

> *I am glad to boast about my weaknesses, so that the power*
> *of Christ may work through me. . . . For when I am*
> *weak, then I am strong. (2 Corinthians 12:7–10 NLT)*

The secret to Paul's powerful leadership and positive role modeling was in recognizing and confessing his weaknesses so the power of Christ could work through him. Christ is the source of your power. Admitting you need help and asking your family to hold you accountable places you in a position for God's power to work through you. He knows your struggles and weaknesses, and in fact, so does your family. Trying to cover them up is futile. It is so much better to own up to your faults and ask for your family's help. Whether you make the right choices or submit to accountability when you make wrong choices, you become an authentic model for your family to follow. The truth is, you can be an excellent model when you make wrong choices simply by exercising humility and confession. Your kids need to see what that looks like too. I have been that kind of model more times than I like to admit.

It was a hectic morning. I had several important meetings lined up, and I was running late. But before I could get out of the bedroom, Dottie began asking me about details I didn't feel I had time to go into. Within seconds we were arguing. Finally, I threw up my hands and said, "I'm out of here." I stormed out the door and drove off.

As I headed down the road, I said to myself, "McDowell, what in the world is up with you? Get yourself back to the house and clear the slate with your wife." I turned around, went back to the house, apologized to Dottie for blowing up, and asked her to forgive me for hurting her.

She, of course, accepted my apology but said, "It's too bad our kids weren't here to see you apologize like this." I asked, "Why?" She said, "We rarely have an argument like we did and our kids don't get to see how we resolve our conflicts."

So later, at dinner, I told the kids how I had been wrong in being so disrespectful to their mother that morning in the bedroom. Even though they didn't see the conflict, it gave me an opportunity to model before my kids what a person should do after making the wrong choice. Openly making yourself accountable to God and to your kids demonstrates that you are a student willing to learn. It also makes you an excellent and effective teacher.

Why Accountability Works

What does it say to your kids when you ask them to hold you accountable for your actions? It says you honor, respect, and value their views and input. It tells them that they are important to you. It also demonstrates humility and repentance. One of the most difficult things for any person to do is humbly confess that he or she is wrong. Yet brokenness is a critical key in teaching our kids right from wrong because all of us make wrong choices, and we need to be broken enough to confess those wrongs.

King David is a good model of one who made wrong choices and humbly sought forgiveness. When David committed his terrible string of multiple sins, God didn't demand that he perform a slew of good deeds to gain forgiveness. The penitent David knew what God wanted from him: "The sacrifices of God are a broken spirit; a broken and contrite heart O God, you will not despise" (Psalm 51:17 NLT). Accountability both models and teaches the heart attitude we must adopt when we make wrong choices.

Not only does accountability demonstrate repentance and make your kids feel valued, it also solidifies in their minds and hearts what is right and wrong. As we have previously noted, today's culture tells our kids that they are to decide for themselves what is right or wrong. Truth is not universal; it is to be subjectively determined. You can go a long way toward reversing that thinking by making yourself accountable to your kids and establishing your household as an accountability family.

In our story, Brad referred to a group that could help provide accountability by tracking his internet activity. This part of our story was not fiction; there is such a group. It is called Covenant Eyes. Presently, Covenant Eyes serves 200,000 members, offering a service that tracks user website visits on computers, smartphones, and tablets and then compiles the data into an easy-to-read report. Each website visited is assigned an age-based rating, such as T for teen or M for mature. The sites and the search terms you use are all listed in the accountability report. The purpose of the report is to enable you and your accountability partner to have a conversation about your internet use. (You can learn more about Covenant Eyes at www.covenanteyes.com.)

Covenant Eyes joined with us in commissioning the Porn Phenomenon Study that we have cited in earlier chapters. When the analysis was done, the researchers compared the views and activities of the general population regarding internet pornography with those of Covenant Eyes accountability families. As you may recall, the study showed that only 32 percent of teens and young adults in America believe that viewing pornography is morally wrong, ranking it almost at the bottom of behaviors they consider harmful.[1] But among the Covenant Eyes accountability families, viewing pornography was ranked at the top as the worst of personal behaviors.[2]

When the survey got specific about what types of pornographic images were morally wrong, the difference was striking. Less than 20 percent of the general population believes viewing same-gender and multipartner sexual acts is always morally wrong. Yet over 90 percent of accountability families say viewing those images is always morally wrong.[3] What percentage of the American general population said pornography is very bad for society? The answer is 45 percent. Yet 99 percent of the Covenant Eyes accountability families said pornography is very bad for society.[4]

Accountability works to help change our kids' attitudes. Why? Because when a young person comes across internet porn, the accountability report makes it a topic of discussion. The very fact that a viewing incident is flagged is an indicator to a young person that something about it is wrong or potentially wrong. The parent/child discussion that ensues then reinforces this view. It gets back to what Moses said to the children of Israel: "Repeat them [the instructions] again and again to your children. Talk about them when you are at home and when you go to bed and when you are getting up" (Deuteronomy 6:7). You simply cannot pass on your values without repeatedly sharing them with your kids. An accountability process gives you the opportunity to systematically voice to your kids the values you hold dear. And over time those values can be embraced by your kids.

When positive values are adopted, positive behavioral changes occur. The study shows that 49 percent of the general population of American teens and young adults seek out porn at least monthly. Among accountability families, that behavior is cut almost in half, with only 26 percent of their young people seeking out porn monthly.[5] The survey found that 41 percent of American young people have sent a nude image to someone via their smartphone, compared to only 14 percent of young people in the accountability families.[6]

Accountability isn't a cure-all. But it exponentially increases your chances of changing your child's attitude and behavior, not only toward internet porn but in other areas as well. Accountability works to teach your kids right from wrong because it gives you the opportunity to talk openly with them about truth, values, behaviors, and morality. It works best when applied intentionally through a systematic process.

The 4 C's Process

The 4 C's is a process that will help you guide your kids to make right choices. As a prerequisite to applying this process, I'm about to recommend something that may seem very strange to you, but please hear me out. When you are given the opportunity to discuss issues of right and wrong with your kids, it's important that you never answer their questions. Don't worry, I don't mean you should leave them hanging when they raise issues about what is right and what is wrong. I'm simply stressing that the process works best when you are the one asking your kids the questions and leading them to discover the answers for themselves. Answers you give them may or may not sink deeply into their psyche. But they will own every answer they discover for themselves. It is their own discovery—a buried treasure they dug up themselves—and they will take it to heart and lock it in. Where do you get the right questions to ask? That is where the 4 C's process comes in.

When I was developing the *Right from Wrong* family of products some two decades ago, my publishing team helped me create the 4 C's process. It is an easy-to-use process designed to teach kids how to determine right from wrong through a series of questions. Hundreds of thousands of families have used and still use this process to help their kids know how to make right moral choices.

The process involves four decision-making steps:

1. Consider the choice;

2. Compare it to God;

3. Commit to God's way; and

4. Count on God's protection and provision.

We will summarize each of these steps in the remainder of this chapter and then explain and illustrate them fully in the following chapters. In those chapters we will continue to follow the saga of the Jefferies family to see how Brad and Aubrey used the 4 C's to lead Jayden to make right choices.

1. Consider the Choice

In a single day, each of us makes literally scores of choices. Most of them are almost automatic. We choose what time to get up in the morning, what clothes to wear, what to eat, what route to take to work or school, where to park, and so on. We take little time considering these choices.

But when it comes to making a moral choice, we need to pause and realize that we are at a crossroads—to selfishly choose our way or defer to God's way. The choices we face—to be less than honest, to spend just a few minutes on a porn site, or for a student to enhance his test score by "borrowing" someone else's answers—are often made without considering the gravity of the decision. Each choice is like a fork in the road, and which option we choose can lead us either upward or downward. A wrong choice may seem trivial at the moment, but it will put you on a wrong path that may lead to difficulties not apparent at the moment of choice. And once a choice is made, turning back is never as easy as one thinks. Making right moral choices is critical, and before we make them we must first pause long enough to remind ourselves that we are facing an option that will lead us either closer to God or further away from Him.

2. Compare the Choice to God

Shortly after the completion of creation, one of the two first humans made a wrong choice with devastating results that have reverberated through time. Eve didn't pause long enough to consider that her choice was self-serving. And to add insult to injury, she failed to compare her choice to God's nature and ways. She didn't take God's view into consideration. That is what healthy relationships do—they take the other person into consideration. In this case, was Eve to believe God had her best interest at heart in denying her a certain fruit? Or was He trying to selfishly keep her from becoming sovereign over her life as He was over His?

What Eve failed to do was to look to God and compare her attitude and action to Him. That would have meant looking at the choice in relation to God's nature and His ways, which were in fact in her best interest. This, of course, would have required that she believe that He was her universal standard for right—not herself.

God's commands come out of His nature, and His nature is holy and right. So when we compare our choices to His nature, it is imperative that we recognize that He is sovereign. Who He is defines what is right, and anything that conflicts with His nature is wrong. When we place our moral choice in the light of the character of God, our decision becomes crystal clear.

3. Commit to God's Way

Committing to God's way is easier said than done. It means we must admit we are not the ruler of our lives—He is. Eve failed to admit this fact, even though it should have been obvious to her. She allowed such self-focused thoughts to obscure what she knew to be true, and thus she chose not to commit to God's way.

Eve's mistake is prevalent in today's world. The concept of deciding what is "right for me" appeals to so many people because it puts self in charge. It permits us to justify our attitudes and actions regardless of how they compare to God's character. Granting ourselves the capacity to decide our own morality makes us feel independent and empowered. That is not an easy temptation to resist. But when we truly believe that God has our best interest at heart, it greatly reduces the difficulty of committing to His ways. That commitment will not only clarify our decisions when faced with right-or-wrong choices; it will also bring into our lives an abundance of physical, emotional, and relational benefits.

4. Count on God's Protection and Provision

Eve's failure to consider the long-term effects of her choice, to compare her choice with God, and to commit to God's way led to her fourth failure. Having allowed herself to be led deeper into temptation by her previous doubts, she finally succumbed when she concluded that God did not have her best interest at heart. She allowed herself to believe the delusion that the prohibition He had placed on her was not for her own good. Why would He deny her a fruit that would open new vistas of power and new knowledge of hidden secrets? It seemed to her that He was not providing for her needs.

When we realize that God is the giver of all the good we have and forbids only what would harm us, we can begin to count on His protection and provision. This realization will open our hearts to discern the difference between right and wrong as never before. It will become clear that right choices lead to our safety and security, whereas wrong choices lead to danger and loss.

Here we must add that making right choices doesn't mean that everything will always be rosy. In fact, God's Word says bluntly that we may be called to suffer for righteousness' sake. However, even such suffering has its rewards. Standing strong in the face of opposition brings many spiritual blessings, such as freedom from guilt, a clear conscience, and the joy of His smile upon our lives.

We can also enjoy many physical, emotional, and relational benefits when we commit to His ways. Of course, His protection and provision should not be the primary motivation for obeying Him; we should obey Him simply because we love Him and trust Him. But the practical and spiritual benefits of obedience certainly provide powerful encouragement for choosing right and rejecting wrong.

If there is any secret to making the right choices in life, it is having the deep conviction that God loves you beyond all comprehension and always wants what is best for you. Lead your kids to believe that with their whole heart, and they will make choices to be honest, live sexually pure lives, love and respect others, show mercy, forgive, and exhibit self-control. Being obedient isn't simply a matter of obligation and duty— it comes out of a deep devotion to the God who loves your kids to death. Literally, to His death on the cross. The more they capture the true vision of who God is, the more they will choose to follow in His ways.

Now that we have summarized the 4 C's process, let's turn back the clock on the Jefferies and see how differently things play out when Brad and Aubrey apply the process in dealing with Jayden's problem.

CHAPTER 7

Consider the Choice

I t was a little past 10:30 p.m. when Aubrey Jefferies slipped quietly into her home. The lights were turned off, so she assumed that Brad and the two children were already in bed. Guided by hallway nightlights, she tiptoed up the stairway and down the hall, hoping she could slip into bed without awakening her husband.

As she made her way past the bedroom of Jayden, their fourteen-year-old son, she thought she heard a muffled sound coming from under the closed door. She stopped to listen. It sounded like the voice of a woman. Aubrey slowly turned the doorknob and peered into the room. Jayden was sitting at his desk with his back to her, staring intently at his computer. Displayed on the screen was a provocative young woman, completely naked, speaking to the viewer in seductive tones.

Aubrey covered her mouth to conceal the sound of her gasp. She slowly closed her son's door and slipped away. Jayden, totally focused on the girl on the screen, never heard a thing. Aubrey tiptoed to her bedroom and touched her husband on the shoulder.

"Brad, wake up!"

"Huh, what. . .what's up?" Brad mumbled without moving.

"It's Jayden," Aubrey began. "I just saw him viewing porn."

Brad turned onto his back. "You saw what?"

"In checking on Jayden, I opened his door and saw that he was on the internet looking at porn."

Brad, now fully awake, sat up in bed. "Did you say anything to him?"

"No. He never even noticed that I opened his door."

Brad took a deep breath. "This is what I feared. I wanted him to be spared that stuff."

Aubrey nodded in agreement. "Yeah, it breaks my heart too. What do you think we should do?"

The couple continued discussing their options and decided to approach Jayden the next evening.

It's Bound to Happen

In today's American culture, your kids face a myriad of temptations, not the least of which is internet porn. As we've stated, 71 percent of teenagers ages thirteen through seventeen come across internet porn without even looking for it.[1] And the cultural thinking of our time does nothing to discourage them from taking the plunge. In fact, the cultural philosophy of the day actually encourages it: "You decide what's right or wrong for you. No one has the right to tell you what you should or should not look at. You are free to choose your own standards and fulfill your own desires."

It's almost as if moral discipline and restraint isn't an option. Modern education teaches our kids that humans are nothing more than a higher form of animal with instinctive cravings that are meant to be satisfied. Your urges are natural because they come from nature, so why should you resist them? Working against this pervasive cultural mind-set, young people like Jayden may feel the opposite tug of parental or religious scruples imploring them not to view the porn so ubiquitously thrust at them. When faced with the choice, they may feel momentarily conflicted. Charles Darwin emphasized this point in his book *The Descent of Man* when he raised the question: "Why should a man feel that he ought to obey one instinctive desire rather than another?"[2] Then he went on to answer the question by saying that when the animalistic human is confronted with competing instinctive desires, "the stronger of the conflicting impulses wins out."[3] By this standard, which is endorsed by the current culture, sexual morality is determined by whatever your stronger drives dictate.

That's what animals do; they follow the strongest instinctive desire. So if a man is nothing more than a high form of animal and has a strong lustful desire to view internet porn or engage in sex with another man's wife, what ought he do? According to the current thinking of the culture, the answer is clear: follow whatever impulse is the strongest. If at the moment his lustful desire for another woman is stronger than his commitment to his wife, then infidelity is the way to go. That's living free; that's being liberated from restrictive religious rules; that's the natural conclusion if humanity evolved from animals without God as the definer of morality.

Jayden and his entire generation have grown up in a culture that has distorted what constitutes true freedom. People who have never given the matter much thought tend to see freedom as doing whatever you feel like doing. They are influenced by the cultural narrative that tells us to follow whichever behavioral drive is strongest at the moment. But when you think it through, there is nothing free about this conclusion. Indeed, it is one of the worst forms of bondage. When you act solely in response to the barrage of impulses fired into you by your base desires, you are not free at all. You are merely a puppet or a slave to your lusts.

Freedom, from a biblical point of view, is something quite

different. Real freedom comes when God frees us from the binding chains of our base desires, giving us the capacity to reject the dominant desire of the moment and choose the right course in the long run. Freedom is the capacity to choose and do what is right. Animals may have no choice but to give in to their strongest instinctive desires, but humans are designed to choose between their instinctive lusts and a universal concept of right defined by their Creator. That is what the first step in making moral decisions, "Consider the Choice," is all about. It helps us understand that we are not animals driven by animalistic instincts. We are humans created in the image of God, with dignity, value, and a moral code from which we can choose right over wrong.

The first task facing Brad and Aubrey is to help Jayden understand his choice. Jayden, like the very first human couple, is tempted to think that right and wrong is something he can determine for himself. But he must learn that humans are not given that prerogative; it belongs solely to God.

A Misconception from the Beginning

Let's go back a good number of millennia to where the misconception about the nature of our choice began. It was the first time in human history that a person did not correctly "consider the choice" before she made it. The instigator of this misconception was Satan himself. In order to show how that original incident reflects the nature of the choices we make today, I've taken the liberty to paraphrase and amplify the account of it that's recorded in Genesis chapter 3.

Satan approached the first lady Eve in the form of a serpent—the perfect disguise to accomplish his deception. Serpents were wise and subtle, and the innocent woman apparently did not yet know enough about creation to think it strange that this creature was endowed with reason and speech. Therefore, she did not suspect a thing as this creature slipped into the Garden of Eden and started a conversation with her.

"I have been watching you, beautiful lady," he said, "and I can't help but wonder why you put up with this relationship God has forced on you."

"What do you mean?" Eve replied.

"Just look at it—the whole relationship between you and God. It's all about what *He* wants. But what about what you want? He's robbing you of your right to make your own choices and express your true identity as a real person."

"Oh, it's not like that at all," replied Eve. "He gives us the run of this garden, and everything He tells us to do makes it clear that He has our best interests at heart. Every command He gives is designed to make us happy." She paused to wrap an ivy tendril around an oak limb. "Why should we want anything different?"

The creature rolled his eyes upward. "That God of yours has really got you fooled. How can you think it's in your best interest when He won't give you the freedom to make your own decisions? He won't even let you decide what you should and should not eat."

"That's not true," said Eve. "God made thousands and thousands of fruits and vegetables, and He allows us to eat all of them. Well, all but one."

"But He did forbid that one fruit, did He not? And what a fruit that is! Just look at it." He pointed to the lush, leafy tree in the center of the garden, its branches heavy with glistening orbs of ripened fruit. "It's the brightest, juiciest, sweetest smelling fruit in the entire garden. Yet that God of yours tells you not to eat it.

If He is so good and has your best interests at heart, why does He withhold such a delicious morsel from you?"

"He said if we ate it we would die."

"Ah, but I happen to know better," replied the forked tongue of Satan. "That fruit won't kill you. Do you want to know the real reason God forbids it?" He leaned close to her ear and lowered his voice to little more than a whisper. "It's because it will make you equal to Him, and He doesn't want rivals. He wants to keep you ignorant so He can control you. If you really want to be like God, you must be independent enough to call your own shots and eat what you want to eat. Let Him know that you won't be kept down any longer. Get an identity of your own—take control of your own destiny. Be your own person. Do your own thing."

The more Eve listened to the smooth-talking serpent, the more God's warning faded and His words became hazy. They didn't seem to make sense anymore. Maybe that snake was right; maybe God didn't have her best interests at heart. Maybe she needed to break free of God to become her own person. With her heart racing, she reached out and gingerly touched her finger to the fruit. Nothing happened. She touched it again, tentatively closing her fingers around its cool, silky skin. Nothing happened. Then she gripped it firmly, pulled it from the tree, and took a quick bite before she could change her mind. Immediately, she ran to Adam and managed to cajole him into eating it with her.[4]

We have devised this amplification of Genesis 3 to help us get to the root of what it means to "consider the choice." If we miscalculate this first step, we fall into Satan's trap and make the wrong choice.

What was the real sin that Adam and Eve committed on that fateful day? Was it that they didn't memorize God's rules about avoiding a particular tree? Was it that they didn't love God enough to do what He asked them to do? Or was it that they didn't trust God enough to believe that the prohibition of the fruit was for their own good? The fact is, they failed in each of these areas, but none of them gives us the complete picture. The central sin behind all others was that of claiming self-sovereignty. They were created to be dependent on and intimately connected to God, but they demanded independence. Eve felt she had the right to determine for herself whether she should eat the fruit that God had forbidden. She chose to be relationally independent of God and to decide what was right for herself. The sad reality is that she never had that right in the first place. She had the right to *choose* right over wrong, but not to decide *what* is right or wrong. Right was already determined by God, and wrong was whatever did not align with right. When Satan came into the Garden, Eve stood at a crossroads. She faced a choice between God's way and her own that would have monumental implications for her and her descendants for the entire span of earthly time. The first step toward making the right decision was simply to "consider the choice" that Satan placed before her: Would she choose God's way or her own?

God and God alone sets the standard for what constitutes all that is right, holy, and true. When Eve chose to disobey God, she took on that role for herself, thus usurping a prerogative belonging only to God. On that count, the serpent was right when he told her, "Your eyes will be opened as soon as you eat it [the forbidden fruit], and you will be like God, knowing both good and evil" (Genesis 3:5). By her act of disobedience, Eve set herself up as her own god.

When Eve took on the task of deciding what was right for

her, she did become her own god. When Adam, Eve, or anyone else decides that they know what is right for themselves, they turn away from the true God and begin worshipping the god of self. Rather than living in relationship with the Creator, they act selfishly as their own god and consequently disconnect from Him. At its core, sin is selfishly choosing our own way in an attempt to fulfill our own desires. The choice we are required to consider is always the same: It's either God's way and a relationship with Him that brings joy and fulfillment, or our own way and a continual separation from Him that results in pain, heartache, suffering, and death.

The Choice Should Be Clear

It was Friday evening, and Jayden's sister was at a friend's home for a sleepover. After dinner, Brad asked if Jayden would join him and Aubrey in the living room.

"Jayden," Brad began, "your mother and I need to discuss a few things with you."

"Okay," Jayden replied as he flopped down on the couch.

"I'd like to make our interaction together as comfortable as possible. But it may be a little uncomfortable at first. Okay?"

"Yeah, I guess so. What's up?"

"I think that's what I'd like to ask you, Buddy," Brad replied. "What's up with some of your late-night internet site visits?"

Jayden looked over at his mom, back to his dad, and then slowly lowered his head. "I don't know."

"I think you do know," Brad continued. "You and I have talked about this before, and I explained my own struggle to stay away from those sites. Do you remember that?"

Jayden nodded, his head still down.

"I explained why it wasn't good for me or anyone else to visit those sites. Do you remember what I said?"

"Something about Mom not wanting you to do that?" Jayden's reply took the form of a question.

"Why do you think I didn't want your Dad to do that, Jayden?" Aubrey asked.

"Dad said you got your feelings hurt or something. Right?" Jayden kept his gaze on the floor, looking at neither Brad nor Aubrey.

"Yeah," Aubrey said softly. "But why do you think it would hurt me? How could Dad looking at porn in private hurt *me*?"

"I don't know for sure."

"It's because it violated God's intent and purpose for sex," Brad explained. "Sex is a wonderful and powerful gift that God gave us to reinforce the relationship between a husband and wife and to bring about the miracle of new life. Because sex is meant to be shared between a husband and wife, God meant it to be intimate, private, and confined totally within the marriage relationship. So when I selfishly spent my sexual energy on images of women who were not my wife, I violated the exclusive intimacy of our marriage relationship. I disrespected your mother, and I disrespected God. It was very selfish of me. I was only thinking about myself. When your mother found out, it really hurt her and our relationship. It was so wrong."

"I've forgiven your Dad, Jayden," Aubrey said, "and we're overcoming the fallout of that disrespect. But honey, I don't want to see you someday suffer through what we've suffered."

"The problem, Jayden," Brad said, "is that I never really stopped to consider my choice. Instead of stopping to consider how God designed sex for a beautiful purpose, I just selfishly shut out that truth and followed my lustful thoughts. Whenever we choose to follow our lustful thoughts, it's always wrong. Does that make sense?"

"Yeah, I guess so," Jayden responded.

"What I'd like to do," Brad continued, "is to take some time with you over the next couple of weeks so you and I can talk through how to resist those temptations, starting with how to detect a selfish choice. Okay?"

"Okay."

"And Jayden," Aubrey added, "I want you to know I'm proud of you and your dad. You're my wonderful son, and your dad is my wonderful husband. God gave me two awesome men in my life, and I love you two with all my heart."

"I love you too, dear," Brad responded.

"Me too, Mom," Jayden said, finally lifting his head to look straight at his mother.

Created for a Purpose

What are Brad and Aubrey attempting to accomplish in their conversation with Jayden? First, they are taking something that Jayden is hiding and bringing it into the light of grace. They are exposing their son's use of internet pornography while avoiding the atmosphere of condemnation. When our kids have done wrong, it is vital that they sense we are there to help lift them up, not to put them down for what they've done.

Second, Brad and Aubrey are emphasizing that selfish choices are wrong choices that always hurt someone—sometimes perhaps only the person making the choice, but often others as well. To avoid making wrong choices, we must stop and consider what we are about to do: Is the choice we are about to make selfishly driven? It may feel good or right at the moment, but is it the right thing to do morally?

Reality is, in the heat of the moment sex feels good no matter if it is morally right or wrong. So we are not going to be very successful in teaching our kids that internet porn or sex before marriage or any moral choice isn't right because it doesn't feel good. They have already been told by numerous outside sources that, for example, sex is great almost anytime. And it is generally portrayed in the media as instant pleasure with few negative consequences. Most wrong choices actually give some sort of immediate pleasure or benefit, while right choices offer a delayed benefit. On the surface, that makes some wrong choices more appealing than right choices.

You will note that the Jefferies chose to make a strong emphasis on the positive benefits of delaying sexual indulgence until it can be exercised within the moral context of marriage. This is not to say we shouldn't point out the negative aspects of wrong choices, we should. But some parents tend to only emphasize the negative consequences that come from indulging in immorality. I suppose those parents and leaders avoid explaining the benefits of doing sex right because they fear that any positive reference to sex will only increase the young person's desire for it. They are afraid to praise the act they want their kids to avoid.

Well, when it comes to sex, our kids already sense and anticipate the pleasure of it. You cannot root that out of their psyches. Peers, entertainment, the media, advertising, and other sources have bombarded them with enticing sexual information and images all their young lives. So, we parents and Christian leaders need to help them understand how much greater and fantastic sex is when experienced with the right person at the right time. That is, of course, with a spouse after a wedding. In other words, when a person engages in sex within the context of God's design for it, then that person can enjoy sex to the max!

When we follow the manufacturer's instructions on how anything is designed to work—that's when it works best. We maximize the benefit of things by using them the way they were designed to be used. And we were designed to do right and to experience life's best by following God's instructions.

Have you ever tried to take a pet fish on a walk, grow a palm tree at the North Pole, or screw a Phillips-head screw in with a conventional screwdriver? You will have problems all the way around. Why? Because fish were not created to take walks. They were designed to live in water, not on land. For a fish to enjoy life as it's meant to be enjoyed, it must live where it was created to live—in water. As for the palm tree and the screwdriver—well, I think you see my point. If animals, plants, and machines are to flourish with maximum efficiency, they must function according to their design. It's just that simple.

Our task as parents and gatekeepers is to help our kids understand that when we resist our selfish desires and choose God's way, we are functioning according to God's design for us. Following God's plan always results in a rewarding purpose. Sex, for example, is designed by God for specific purposes. It deepens a married couple's love life, brings joy and physical pleasure into their relationship, and creates a loving family of one or more children. When we respect and honor sex for how it was meant to be used, sex becomes one of the best things God created.

Choosing God's way is always good. We were created in His

image, and aligning ourselves to that image enables us to live as we were meant to live—happy and fulfilled. Considering the choice is only the first step in teaching our kids how to make right choices. The next step is actually comparing our choice to God. That is the subject of the following chapter.

CHAPTER 8

Compare It to God

Brad and his son Jayden strolled through the local park, sometimes passing mothers herding small children and sometimes moving over to allow a jogger to trot by. "Yes, Jayden," Brad was saying, "my consistent viewing of porn did hurt your mom, but there's more to it than that. Think with me here. What was it that I was really failing to do?"

Jayden thrust his hands in his pockets as he mulled over the question. He seemed to understand that his dad's use of porn was selfish, and it had hurt his mom. But Brad wanted to lead his son to realize exactly why it was wrong.

"Was it that you failed to be honest with Mom?"

"Sure, that's part of it. I wasn't being open and transparent with her. But there was a principle I violated. Something I promised your mother on our wedding day."

"Oh, I know." Jayden pointed his finger in the air to signal he'd figured it out. "You said you'd be faithful to her and you weren't, sort of. Right?"

"Right. Not only did my use of porn show disrespect for your mom, it also showed that I was hedging on my wedding vow. I wasn't having an affair with another woman per se, yet I wasn't really being faithful to her as I promised. My sin was lust for images of women that were not my wife, and that violated God's principle of faithfulness. Does that make sense?"

"Yeah, it does."

"Okay, now hang with me here, because here comes the most

important part." Brad put his hand on Jayden's shoulder as the two continued to walk. "The Bible warned me that unfaithfulness to my wife is wrong. In the Old Testament book of Malachi 2:16 I am told to 'Guard your heart; do not be unfaithful to your wife.' But do you know why unfaithfulness is wrong?"

"I guess because the Bible says it is."

"That's what a lot of people think, but there's more to it than that. The Bible does say unfaithfulness is wrong, but that isn't what makes it wrong. There is something else. And buddy, this is the big one. If you can get this one principle into your head, you will understand how to determine what's truly right and wrong so you can make right and life-giving choices every time."

"What is it?" Jayden stopped and looked at his dad. "What's the big one?"

Brad knew he had finally caught his son's attention. He pointed to a park bench, "Let's sit down a minute." As the two sat, Brad stretched out his son's curiosity a little longer. "So what do you think it is, Jayden? What is that one, big thing that makes lust and unfaithfulness wrong?"

"Uh, selfishness?" came the reply.

"Well, selfishness leads to lust and unfaithfulness, that's for sure. But there's something else that makes it wrong. Actually, it isn't a something; it's a somebody."

"God?" Jayden ventured with a tone of doubt.

"You're right, up to a point," affirmed Brad. "The big thing that makes unfaithfulness wrong is something about God, something in His nature." He could tell by the blank look on his son's face that he wasn't getting it. "Okay, let me ask you this. Remember when you were running that cross-country race last year?"

"Yeah."

"When that Chad Brooks kid intentionally knocked you down and you lost the race, something inside told you that what he did was wrong. What was that something inside you?"

"Anger! Man, it really made me mad."

Brad laughed at the memory. "Yeah, you were mad alright. But there was something else inside you that made you know that what Chad did to you was wrong. It was a sense of fairness and justice which you knew had been violated, right?"

"Yeah, I felt that. I definitely did."

"Well, that sense of justice was placed inside you by God Himself, because He created you in His image. A sense of justice and fairness is standard equipment for every one of us, and it comes from God. We have that sense of fairness and justice because God had it first. He is a just God by nature. And when He created us in His image, He passed it on to us. The fact that a virtue resides within God is what makes it right at the core. A thing is right not merely because it's commanded in the Bible; it's commanded in the Bible because it is right. What is right always has its roots deep in the character and nature of God Himself. Does that make sense?"

"Sure," came the reply.

"So, what is there about God that makes being unfaithful wrong?"

Jayden thought for a moment. "I really don't know, Dad. What is it?"

"Well," Brad began, "God by His very nature is true. Being true and faithful is a facet of His unchangeable nature. He doesn't break His promises. And here I am, created in His image, designed to reflect the nature of God who is true and faithful. And what did I do? I was unfaithful to your mom with my porn use. But Jayden"—Brad paused to take a deep breath—"first and foremost, I sinned against my true and faithful God. He's been so faithful to me, and I wasn't faithful to Him or your mom."

Jayden looked at his dad and saw tears welling up in his eyes. He reached over and touched Brad on the arm.

"It's okay, Dad. I'm sure God's forgiven you."

"Yeah, He has son. He's really faithful like that to me. And to you too."

Tracing Morality Back to the Person of God

What was Brad trying to teach his son? He was identifying what makes sexual immorality wrong by tracing a human offense from the precept to the principle to the person of God. In a previous chapter, we showed that God's commands are structured on three successive levels. The first level is the command, which is called the *Precept*. The second level is the basis for the command, or the *Principle*, which the command upholds. The third level is the bedrock source of the command, which is always rooted in the *Person of God*. Brad addressed the human offense of sexual unfaithfulness and showed his son why it is so offensive by explaining how it violates who God is and how He created us to be. It is wrong not merely because it is a command, but because it is inconsistent with the character of God. We know an offense is universally wrong when it runs contrary to the nature of God.

Many Precepts

The Bible leaves no room for ambiguity in its denunciation of sexual immorality, which includes all sex that occurs outside of a marriage (extramarital and premarital sex). Here are a few passages that warn us against sexual sin:

- "You must abstain from. . .sexual immorality" (Acts 15:29).
- "Run from sexual sin!" (1 Corinthians 6:18).
- "We must not engage in sexual immorality" (1 Corinthians 10:8).
- "Among you there must not be even a hint of sexual immorality. . .because these are improper for God's holy people" (Ephesians 5:3 NIV).
- "God's will is for you to be holy, so stay away from all sexual sin" (1 Thessalonians 4:3).

The Bible writers are united in presenting sexual morality as a command. But these commands rest on at least two very important principles, one of faithfulness and purity. And those two valued principles come directly from the very person and character of God.

The Origin of Faithfulness

The seventh of the Ten Commandments is "You must not commit adultery" (Exodus 20:14). Jesus affirmed this commandment when He made the point that once a man and woman are united in marriage, they are not to commit adultery but remain faithful to one another. He said, "Let no one split apart what God has joined together" (Mark 10:9). God told Israel, "I hate divorce! . . . So guard your heart; do not be unfaithful to your wife" (Malachi 2:16).

On their wedding day, Brad and Aubrey made a vow of commitment to be faithful to one another..."to have and to hold, from this day forward: for better, for worse; for richer, for poorer; in sickness and in health; to love and to cherish till death do us part. And hereto I pledge you my faithfulness." Perhaps nothing is more rewarding than to sense that someone loves you more than any other and will devote himself or herself to you for life. Faithfulness is God's cherished principle designed to provide Brad and Aubrey with a sex life filled with maximum joy and pleasure and to protect them from the negative consequences of sexual immorality.

As egregious as sexual unfaithfulness is, the hurt that it causes a couple is not what makes it wrong. This is an important point because many of our kids define wrong solely on the basis of the harm it does to another person. We've all heard it: "Hey, what's the problem with what I'm doing if it isn't hurting anyone?" Based on that standard, Brad's internet porn use would not be wrong as long as his wife didn't find out. An extramarital affair would not be wrong as long as it remained secret. Pornography use and sexual affairs suddenly become wrong as soon as someone gets hurt. That "logic" describes the moral approach adopted by much of the current generation.

It's true that selfish actions that hurt other people are wrong. But what makes it morally wrong finds its genesis in the nature of God. As Brad explained to Jayden, God, by His very nature, is faithful. It is His innate characteristic of faithfulness that causes Him to care so much about whether we are faithful. Our actions are judged to be right or wrong, moral or immoral based on whether they reflect His image. And God so wants us to reflect His image—which is for our best—that He gets jealous when we don't.

The Bible expresses this extreme care that God displays for us in terms of jealousy, which often causes us confusion. When God gave Moses the Ten Commandments—His precepts designed to guide the people into moral actions—He said, "I, the LORD your God, am a jealous God" (Exodus 20:5). At first this may seem confusing. The word *jealous* in English is generally used in a negative sense, meaning something akin to envy or covetousness. But the two words "jealous God" in the Hebrew are *el qanna*, which denotes passion and zeal. It expresses God's devotion and passion for His beloved nation of Israel. God considered the children of Israel to be His marriage partner. He loved them with the devotion of a husband to his wife, and He wanted them to love Him as a wife devoted to her husband. He wanted the relationship to be exclusive, as a marriage should be. That is why He commanded them to worship no other god but Him. He wants to be loved with a pure and passionate love reserved only for Him.

We were created in God's image, which means that we too have the longing to be that "one and only" to another person. That desire came to us directly from the relational nature of God, who created us to be like Him. Our godlikeness does not include all the characteristics of God: we are not all-powerful, omnipresent, all-knowing, unchanging, or infinite. But we are created in His relational image. He created us in the relational tandem of male and female and placed within each sex a longing for a physical connection, an emotional connection, a bonding of the inner spirit, and an intimate attachment of the soul. Using the device of sexuality, God planted deep within humans an identifying marker or distinguishing characteristic of His own image—the capacity for loving relationships.

God is relational by His very nature. He is three distinct persons—Father, Son, and Holy Spirit—blended in perfect harmony. God has eternally existed in relationship. The Father has always infinitely loved the Son and the Holy Spirit. The Son has always infinitely loved the Father and the Holy Spirit. The Holy Spirit has always infinitely loved the Father and the Son. The Godhead has forever experienced a continuous cycle of perfect relationship.

Although God is the infinite one and we humans are finite, we bear His relational DNA. We have inherited His relational ability to love and be intimate with another, to show mercy and compassion, to be faithful and true, to be fair and just, to be pure and upright, etc. We were created in His image, crafted to reflect, glorify, and magnify our Creator. Scripture says we were designed so "we can be mirrors that brightly reflect the glory of the Lord. And as the Spirit of the Lord works within us, we become more and more like him" (2 Corinthians 3:18 TLB). We are to walk in God's relational image and bear the fruit of his Spirit of "love, joy, peace, patience, kindness, goodness, faithfulness, gentleness, and self-control" (Galatians 5:22–23).

When husbands and wives are commanded to be faithful to one another, they are being instructed to live out the faithful image of God. "Understand. . .that the LORD your God is indeed God," Moses told the Israelites. "He is the faithful God who keeps his covenant for a thousand generations" (Deuteronomy 7:9). "I, the LORD, speak only what is true and declare only what is right" (Isaiah 45:19).

We know that faithfulness in marriage is right and infidelity is wrong not merely because the Bible instructs us accordingly, but because God is faithful by nature. Accurately reflecting the image of God is the true basis for morality, and this is what we want to convey to our kids. We want to make it clear to them that when a husband or wife acts unfaithfully, it is wrong because they are not reflecting the faithful image of God. It is the relational image of God that defines for us what is right.

The Origin of Purity

Purity is another of God's cherished principles that provides couples with a sex life of maximum joy and protects them from the negative consequences of sexual immorality. The Bible says, "Marriage should be honored by all, and the marriage bed kept pure" (Hebrews 13:4 NIV). "God's will is for you to be holy, so stay away from all sexual sin. Then each of you will control his own body and live in holiness and honor—not in lustful passion. . . . God has called us to live holy lives, not impure lives" (1 Thessalonians 4:3–5, 7).

What does it mean to be pure? Have you ever eaten a candy bar that identified itself on the wrapper as "pure milk chocolate"? You've probably seen a label on a jar of honey that read, "Pure honey—no artificial sweeteners." The word *pure* on these product labels means there is no foreign substance added—no preservatives, no artificial flavoring or coloring, no extenders to make the bar larger or the jar fuller. Every bite you take contains nothing but chocolate or honey.

To be pure sexually is to "live according to God's original design." Sex was designed to be expressed between one husband and one wife. To have more than one sexual partner would be to bring a foreign substance into the relationship, which would render the relationship impure. If you drop a dirty pebble into a glass of pure water, the water becomes adulterated—impure. A glass of water that contains no impurities is an unadulterated glass of water. God wants our sex lives to be unadulterated.[1]

Jayden is unmarried, of course, which means he was not being unfaithful to a spouse when he indulged in porn and solicited nude photos from his girlfriend. Yet he was being sexually impure. God designed sex to be experienced within an unbroken circle, a pure union between two virgins entering an exclusive marriage relationship. That pure union can be broken even *before* marriage if one or both partners have not kept the marriage bed pure by waiting to have sex until it can be engaged within the purity of a husband-wife relationship.

Does that sound foreign to the cultural thinking of today? Sure it does. Most Americans accept premarital sex as normal. The prevailing sentiment is, "If a teenage boy and girl feel that they are ready for sex and use proper protection, what's wrong with it?" But feeling ready and using protection have nothing to do with whether premarital sex is right or wrong. That is determined by how the act squares with the character of God.

The very essence of God is purity and holiness. "He is your Redeemer," the prophet Isaiah wrote, "The Holy One of Israel" (Isaiah 54:5). God says, "Be holy, for I am holy" (1 Peter 1:16 NASB). "All who have this hope in him purify themselves, just as he [God] is pure" (1 John 3:3 NIV). God by His very nature is holy and pure. "There is no evil in him" (Psalm 92:15). There is no room for deceit or unclean thoughts within God. There is no reason to doubt or mistrust the purity of His nature. There is nothing in God but openness, pure intentions, and unadulterated love. There are no masks or facades. Nothing stands between you and Him to hinder a close attachment or obstruct an intimate connection.

He is pure of heart and holy in character. With God you can have an ever-deepening relationship untarnished by unfaithfulness and unadulterated by impurity.

That is the kind of relationship you can establish with a loved one when you choose to shun immorality and reflect God's character. You were made in His pure image to live in purity with others. That purity is a critical ingredient in developing a deepened and trusting relationship between a man and a woman. Without it, the relationship will be adulterated and eventually deteriorate into mistrust, disrespect, and betrayal.

Jayden needs to understand that while His impure thoughts and immoral actions may seem private and harmless, they spawn a noxious swamp of mistrust, disrespect, and betrayal. Such behavior leads inevitably to disrupted and destructive relationships. Sexual impurity is wrong and sexual purity right because we were created to reflect the image of a pure God.

Recognizing our selfish tendencies, considering our choice, and then comparing that choice to God is critical in determining what is right and wrong. Yet knowing what is right is one thing, while actually doing it is another matter. Living lives that reflect God's relational image doesn't come naturally in this fallen world of ours. Our next task as parents and Christian leaders is to lead our kids to commit to living lives that accurately reflect the character of God. Read on.

CHAPTER 9

Commit to God's Ways

*J*ayden, wedged on the church pew between his parents, fidgeted as soft music from the church organ filled the sanctuary. "When's this thing going to be over?" he asked.

"Shhh, lower your voice," Aubrey punctuated her command with an elbow to his ribs.

"It won't be too long, Son," Brad responded. "Weddings don't take very long. But of course, there's the reception too."

"That's when we get to eat, right?" Jayden asked.

"Yeah, there'll be food, punch, cake, and all that good stuff. So just endure the ceremony and your patience will be rewarded."

Soon the organ struck the loud opening chord of the wedding processional. The audience stood and turned to watch the bride make her way to the front of the church where her smiling groom waited.

The ceremony proceeded, and as it reached a certain point Brad nudged Jayden. "Listen carefully to this part," he said. "I want to talk to you about it later."

"Okay."

The minister looked to the groom. "Repeat after me. 'I Brandon, take thee Marci, to be my wedded wife.'"

"I Brandon, take thee Marci, to be my wedded wife. . .to have and to hold from this day forward. . .for better or for worse. . .for richer, for poorer. . .in sickness and in health. . .I pledge you my love from this day forward until death do us part."

As the couple exchanged their vows, Jayden listened carefully, just as his dad had instructed. Later when the reception was in full swing, Brad pulled his son aside. "Jayden, did you listen to the vows Brandon and Marci made to each other?"

"Yeah, I did."

"Well, there's a principle within the marriage vows that I've found to be the real power behind me no longer viewing that internet junk. And I think you're ready to discover it too."

"Discover what?"

"I think you're ready to discover the real key to resisting the temptation to view internet porn."

"I thought the key was being accountable to each other," Jayden responded.

"Sure, accountability is huge. But there's something deeper, something at the heart level that keeps us sexually pure. And it has to do with the marriage vows."

"Okay, Dad, just tell me already."

"It's going to take a little bit of unpackaging, which we can do sometime this week. But until then, I want to give you a question to think about." Brad leaned in toward Jayden and spoke softly. "What did the bride and groom mean when they said to each other, 'I pledge you my love'?"

"What?" Jayden asked as he pulled away from Brad. "What does it mean to what?"

"I'm saying the key in having freedom from that internet stuff is understanding what it really means to 'pledge you my love.' Just think about that and we'll talk about it later."

"I Pledge You My Love"

What Brad wants Jayden to discover is what every parent, youth worker, and pastor wants both young and old alike to discover. It's that committing to God's way and living in obedience to Him isn't about trying harder; it's about loving deeply.

Trying harder to live right—staying away from internet porn, putting a stop to lust, ceasing to take selfishly from others, being giving and kind, etc.—can so often be about following rules by sheer human strength and willpower. But the true key to living right is to learn and apply what it means to love God.

When a young man and woman standing before the minister say, "I pledge you my love," what are they saying? Do they mean, "I'll do my best to follow your rules, to always obey you, and to do whatever you say"? No. They are pledging themselves to always be there for each other because they love each other.

Teaching our kids to consider their choice and compare it to God doesn't mean much unless we follow it up with the next step—to commit to His ways and do what is right. This is where the rubber meets the road. This is where their choice to do right is lived out. But our kids need to know that the motivation and power to do the right thing grows out of a deep love and commitment to God. Resisting wrong and choosing right isn't simply about accountability and willpower. It's about the power of love that unleashes the Holy Spirit in our lives.

Many parents and church leaders place a strong emphasis on spiritual discipline and accountability as the primary factors in resisting evil and making right choices. Discipline and accountability are critically important, but they are not the key to living a victorious life in God's Spirit. Unless we place discipline and accountability squarely within a devoted love relationship with God, we will tend to convey a self-effort/try harder message to our kids.

The apostle Paul warned us against this "try harder to follow the rules" message in his letter to the Christians in Galatia who were confused about what it took to live a Spirit-empowered life: "After starting your new lives in the Spirit, why are you now trying to become perfect by your own human effort?. . . I ask you again, does God give you the Holy Spirit and work miracles among you because you obey the law?" (Galatians 3:3, 5). Paul was explaining that trying harder isn't what unleashes God's power in our lives. It's our pledge to love Him and then depend on Him that sets us free to follow in His ways.

When we pledge our love to God, He responds by empowering us with His Holy Spirit. He wants our obedience, of course, but first and foremost He wants *us*. He wants us as a devoted lover who is willing to give ourselves to Him. That is why we are told to "follow the Spirit's leading in every part of our lives" (Galatians 5:25); "Do not let any part of your body become an instrument of evil to serve sin. Instead, give yourselves completely to God" (Romans 6:13); and "Every child of God defeats the evil world by trusting Christ to give the victory" (1 John 5:4 NLT). It is the giving of ourselves to the Holy Spirit that allows His power and presence to be seen through our lives. Paul said, "this light and power that now shine within us—is held in perishable containers, that is, in our weak bodies. So everyone can see that our glorious power is from God and is not our own" (2 Corinthians 4:7 NLT). As weak as we feel at times, if we give ourselves to God He will empower us to live a life pleasing to Him.

The Pledge

Jayden held the forty-gallon plastic bag to the ground while his father raked the first pile of leaves into it. "Well, Jayden," said Brad, "have you thought about what the vow, 'I pledge my love' has to do with resisting porn?"

"Yeah, I thought about it, but I don't really get it."

"Okay, you know I love your mom, right?"

"Yeah."

"On our wedding day, I pledged my love to her, just like our friends Marci and Brandon did. Because I loved her, I said I would give myself to her. That meant her interests would become my interests. Her concerns would become my concerns. In pledging my love, I was saying I wanted to please her in every way I could and make her happy. Does that make sense?"

"Yeah, I get that. If you love someone, you want to make 'em happy."

"Right. So when we make that kind of love pledge to God, something really powerful happens." Brad held the rake against the top of the bag as Jayden set it upright.

"Okay, here's the point," Brad continued as they strolled to the next leaf pile. "After I messed up by viewing internet porn, I recommitted my love to your mom and to God. I told God I wanted to give all of myself to Him, that His interests would be my interests, that His concerns would be mine, and that I wanted to please Him in everything I did."

"How did that change anything?" asked Jayden.

"Since I made that pledge, God's empowering Spirit has given me the strength to resist internet porn. Accountability to others helps, but the Holy Spirit responds to my love pledge with the power to resist temptation. It is His power that keeps me away from porn and has kept me from getting addicted to it. Do you see how that works?"

"Yeah, I sorta do. Because you love God, He loves you back and gives you power to resist wrong things?" It was more a question than a statement.

"Right, you've got it. The great thing about God's love is that it comes with bonuses. Not only does He give me power to live free of porn, He also lets me know He doesn't condemn me. He accepts me and forgives me when I do blow it. He is patient and loving. And that just makes me want to love Him even more."

Brad put his arm around his son. "We have an amazing God, don't we? And He's there to love and empower you too. Isn't that great?"

"Yeah, Dad, that's pretty great!"

"Okay, pull out another bag. Your mom will think we're pretty great if we get these leaves bagged up before dinner."

What Kind of God Do Your Kids See?

In the conversation above, Brad is helping his son connect God's love with God's empowerment to make right choices. That is why the first two steps of the process are so important. When we consider our moral choices and compare them to God, it reveals the heart of a loving God who wants to protect us, provide for us, and sets us free to live fulfilled and happy lives. The purpose of those first two steps is to introduce our kids to a God who wants nothing more than what Jesus stated, "that my joy may be in you and that your joy may be complete" (John 15:11 NIV).

God wants us to enjoy Him, enjoy life, and enjoy each other. The purpose of every rule and instruction He gave us is to provide for our best interests and protect us from harm. Our success in teaching our kids right from wrong and committing to God's ways depends largely on how well we instill into them the picture of a loving God who wants what is best for them. Understanding the true nature of God makes it far more likely that they will commit to Him.

Our kids need to know that God loves them unconditionally. He loves them even before they love Him. "This is real love," John wrote. "Not that we loved God, but that he loved us" (1 John 4:10). That truth is profound. God does not insist that we turn our lives around and live morally before He loves us. He loves us anyway, and He longs for us to return that love so that we can find fulfillment of our purpose when He places His Holy Spirit in our lives. This is why we can say that if we teach our kids to love God, He will empower them to make right choices that lead to living a moral life that reflects His nature.

In chapter 5 we noted that God is not interested in inflicting shame and condemnation on us. He is a loving God who accepts and forgives us. We need to lead our kids to see that He loves us unconditionally, no matter what we have done. This is sometimes a difficult task because so many of us have grown up without such a positive view of God. Often our perception of Him is colored by our past child-parent relationships, especially the relationship with our father.

For example, you may have grown up with an inattentive father, as I did, and you may have felt relationally distant from him. Or perhaps you had somewhat of authoritarian parents, and the dominant vibe you felt from them was disapproval. It is not unusual for people to subconsciously project those negative feelings toward parents into their relationship with God, causing them to see Him as a disapproving or distant father figure. What view of God are you projecting to your kids? How they see God will greatly impact their desire to commit to His ways.

To help us correctly adjust our perception of God, let's travel back to the time when God's Son lived on earth. We will look into the upper room where the Passover meal, often referred to as the Last Supper of Jesus, is in progress. Now imagine you, your family, along with the Jefferies, are seated across the table from Jesus there in the upper room. He first looks your way, and you make eye contact with the Master as He says, "If you love Me, you will keep My commandments" (John 14:15 NASB). What would be your response to His statement? What would go on in kids' minds as to the reason He would be saying these words?

Is Jesus Disappointed?

Jayden's first response to Jesus' words might be to think, *He is disappointed in me.* He would probably hear Jesus through his feelings of shame. In his mind's eye, he would see Jesus crossing His arms and shaking His head, saying, "If you really loved me, young man, you would not have viewed internet porn. Your failures to do the right thing speaks volumes. Jayden, you are such a disappointment to me." How do you respond to Jesus' words? Do you see a disappointed Jesus?

Those who sense God's disappointment in their failures sometimes tend to compensate by working harder at performing for God in hopes of making themselves worthy of His love. The problem is, no one can live the Christian life perfectly. Those who sense a disappointed Jesus will tend to see His love as a meritorious reward for good performance. This will often cause them to see only the "thou shalt nots" of the Bible and miss its many promises. This view sets up their emotions to feel, *I must do right to be loved right.* And invariably, this perception will permeate all their relationships.

Is Jesus Inspecting Us?

If Aubrey had maintained the attitude she projected when we first met her in our first scenario, she might have heard Jesus' words in an altogether different way. She might have seen Him raising his eyebrows and stressing the first word: "*If* you love Me, you will keep My commandments." She would have heard a questioning tone in His voice, as if He were issuing a warning: "Do you realize that I'm watching you to see if you keep my commandments?" This is how Aubrey previously saw God. Consequently, she took on the role of an inspector who suspiciously monitored the behavior of Jayden. Her scrutinizing, inspecting eye sapped the joy out of her relationship with her son.

Far too many people see God in just this way—as an inspector who is grading them on how well they follow His commands. Is that the kind of God you or your kids see? One who stands over you with a pad and pencil, keeping a running tally of all your deeds, both good and bad?

Is Jesus Distant?

Brad may have seen how deeply Jesus was involved with His disciples in this last meal with them, and he may have felt that he was not as close to Jesus as they were. Maybe when Jesus looked at him and said, "If you love Me, you will keep My commandments," Brad saw it as an afterthought without much real thought or attention behind it. It was as if he saw Brad and thought he should say something meaningful, so he threw out a little command in an "oh, by the way" manner. Brad subconsciously saw God as only having time for the "important people" who are doing the "important things" in life. God was disconnected from him, so he was able to disconnect God's command from his secret life. God's attention was elsewhere, so Brad's little private sin wouldn't be noticed.

This distant view of God allows us to disconnect actions that ought to be integrated. If we think God is distant, it's easy to ignore His commands when temptation draws us toward wrong choices. When God is distant, so are His commands. When God is distant, so are His promises, which dulls our anticipation of what He has in store for us in the future. Therefore, I will do what benefits me at the moment and worry about the future when it comes. A distant God has little relevance to our lives.

Jesus Is Accepting and Noncondemning

The reality is, scripture reveals Jesus as a person who sees you just the way you are and loves and accepts you beyond your wildest dreams. Imagine you and your family are again seated across from Him as revealed in John 14. He tells you there are many rooms in His Father's house, and He is going to prepare a place for you. Then He makes all of you a promise—"I will come and get you, so that you will always be with me where I am" (John 14:3).

Jesus then explains that the works He has done were actually not of His own doing: it was the Father working through Him.

So He makes another promise—"Anyone who believes in me will do the same works I have done" (John 14:12).

He smiles reassuringly and gives yet another promise: "You can ask for anything in my name, and I will do it" (John 14:13). You may have committed sins just as the Jefferies family has. You may have felt that He was disappointed in you, inspecting you, or distant from you just as they did. But just look at these promises! None of them sound like they are coming from a disappointed or inspecting or distant Jesus, do they? They are coming from a Jesus who welcomes you and receives your family with a full embrace without reservations or conditions.

Then in a tender voice and with accepting eyes, He makes a final promise. Listen to His words as He extends His arms toward your young people and with a smile on His face says, "If you love Me, you will keep My commandments" (John 14:15 NASB).

This verse involves a promise too. It is the prelude to a very special promise. Notice what Jesus goes on to say in the next two verses: "And I will ask the Father and he will give you another Advocate, who will never leave you. He is the Holy Spirit, who leads into all truth" (John 14:16–17). What a promise! It brings reassurance, security, and confidence to you and your family's heart. Jesus is in effect saying to you and each of your children individually, "If you and I have a loving relationship, I promise I am not going to leave you alone to try harder to commit to my ways. I'm going to take up residence in your life through the power and person of my Holy Spirit, and I will be there to set you free to choose right. Consider your choices, compare them to me, but don't try to commit to my ways in your own strength. I will be your strength. I pledge my love to you. Pledge your love to me and my desires will become your desires, my ways will become your ways."

This is the promise that comes to you and your family from the accepting Jesus. When we embrace this promise, His love becomes real to us. In fact, it is His transforming love that enables us to love Him back so deeply and to love each other as He loves us.

Leading our kids to commit to God's ways becomes a realistic goal when they come to see the real Jesus. The God we serve is not a hard taskmaster that demands obedience and imposes penalties on all who fall short. God is our loving Father, Jesus is our caring brother, and the Holy Spirit is our friend and the one who empowers us.

Listen to Jesus as He offers Himself to those who feel weak and heavily burdened with all their "trying harder" efforts. "Come to me," He says, "all you who are weary and burdened, and I will give you rest. Take my yoke upon you and learn from me, for I am gentle and humble in heart, and you will find rest for your souls" (Matthew 11:28–29 NIV).

The yoke Jesus refers to here isn't a heavy single harness used in olden days to hitch an animal to a plow. He's referring to a dual harness like those that link two oxen together. His yoke binds you and the Holy Spirit together, enabling the two of you to plow through any temptation or problem that looms in your path. Committing to His ways is about loving and learning how to live the kind of life He designed all of us to live. As we love God and follow in His ways, He reinforces His love for us through His protection and provision.

Right moral choices are made when our kids consider the choice, compare the choice to God, and then commit to His loving ways. When we make the right moral choices, we soon find those choices are validated by blessings. These blessings are not rewards that come because God is keeping score and awarding prizes to those who follow His commands. The blessings of obedience come by way of the law of natural consequences. We receive joy and happiness when we follow in God's ways because we were created in His image to live that way. When we live as we were meant to live, blessings follow naturally.

Infusing that reality into our children creates a powerful motivation for them to follow in God's way. That is the topic of the next chapter.

CHAPTER 10

Count on God's Provision and Protection

We've got a twenty-minute ride to where we'll pick up your sister." Brad glanced at Jayden sitting in the back seat. "How about sharing with Mom some of what we've been dealing with together?"

"Ah, I don't know Dad, that may be a bit awkward."

"Well, it doesn't have to be," Brad responded. "Why don't you just share some of the positive stuff about not viewing porn that we talked about the other day?"

"Yeah, I'd like to hear that, Jayden," Aubrey shifted in her seat to see her son more clearly.

"Well. . . I'm not grounded anymore, that's a *big* plus."

"That's certainly a good thing," Aubrey responded. "I'm sure proud of you."

"Let's see, what else," Jayden pondered. "Oh, I'm not sneaking around anymore and feeling guilty about it."

"That's good—a clear conscience," Brad affirmed. "What else?"

"Uhh. . . I don't know. Maybe I'm not watching things that are a little twisted and kinky. That's a positive, right?"

"It sure is," Brad said emphatically. "God never intended sex to be portrayed as it is on those sites. It gives people the wrong idea about the true nature of sex. Sex is a beautiful thing, and they distort it."

"Those are great insights, Jayden," Aubrey said. "In the future, you're going to be so glad you are free of all that stuff. Because one day, when you get married, you'll be able to enjoy the kind of intimate relationship with your new wife that God intended."

"Yeah, Son," Brad added, "you'll be able to enjoy a great relationship without damaging images coming between you and the person you love."

"Jayden, your dad is a living example of how wonderful a relationship can be when porn is not a part of it." Aubrey smiled warmly at her husband. "I'm so proud of both of you."

"I'm proud of me too," Jayden responded as both of his parents laughed.

For Our Own Good

In the scene described above, Brad and Aubrey are attempting to reinforce to their son that following God's ways is not only morally right, but also good for us. Throughout these pages, we've been hammering the principle that when we obey God's instructions, we can count on His protection and provision.

"I know the plans I have for you," God told the nation of Israel, "they are plans for good and not for disaster, to give you a future and a hope" (Jeremiah 29:11). He went on to express His desire for His children to have "one heart and one purpose to worship me forever, for their own good and for the good of all their descendants" (Jeremiah 32:39). Choosing God's way over what seems to be a more appealing wrong way does not sap all the fun and excitement out of life; on the contrary, it accomplishes our created purpose, which is to reflect the likeness and image of God. When we live godly lives—lives that reflect the character of God—we inevitably experience fulfillment, meaning, and true joy. Paradoxically, joy doesn't come from seeking joy. As the title of C.S. Lewis' spiritual autobiography, *Surprised by Joy*, indicates, true joy comes from the last place critics of God's laws would think to look. It comes from seeking God and following His ways.

King David clearly understood that it is beneficial to follow in God's ways:

> *How joyful are those who fear [honor] the LORD and delight in obeying his commands. (Psalm 112:1)*

> *There is joy for those who deal justly with others and always do what is right. (Psalm 106:3)*

In Jesus' great discourse called the Beatitudes, He enumerates the ways in which God blesses those who follow God's ways:

> *God blesses those who are poor and realize their need for him. . .*
> *God blesses those who mourn. . .*
> *God blesses those who are humble. . .*
> *God blesses those who hunger and thirst for justice. . .*
> *God blesses those who are merciful. . .*
> *God blesses those whose hearts are pure. . .*
> *God blesses those who work for peace. . .*
> *God blesses those who are persecuted for doing right. . .(Matthew 5:3–10)*

As Jesus' Beatitude message and His own experience indicates, following God's ways does not prevent a person from encountering difficulty and suffering. Therefore, we must take care not to give the impression that bad things do not happen to moral people, or that people who engage in immorality are never happy. The prophet Jeremiah understood this when he asked, "Why are the wicked so prosperous? Why are evil people so happy?" (Jeremiah 12:1). King David confessed that he had seen "wicked and ruthless people flourishing like a tree in its native soil" (Psalm 37:35).

Living in God's ways is not always immediately rewarded, nor is ungodly living always immediately punished. In fact, sin does promise immediate satisfaction, and it does often deliver pleasure for a period of time. More often than not, however, the rewards of morality and the consequence of immorality will eventually become apparent in this life. But not always. Some of these rewards and consequences may not be measured out until after this life is over.

It's worth repeating that God's ways are not right because they are beneficial to us. They are right because they reflect the rightness of God Himself. To illustrate this point, think back to when you were taught the multiplication tables in the third or fourth grade. That knowledge has paid off many times over for you. It helps you complete your tax return and compare prices in the grocery store. You might say that you get something good from your relationship with the multiplication tables.

But $5 \times 6 = 30$ is not true *because* you get something good out of it. It is true because it is true, because it reflects certain laws. It reflects mathematical reality. The benefit you derive from having learned the multiplication tables is not what makes those facts true; they are true whether you benefit from them or not. But as you make use of the truth of the multiplication tables, you indeed gain benefit.

Similarly, God's ways are not true and right *because* of any benefit you may derive from them; they are true and right because they are rooted in the very essence of who God is. Scripture tells us that God is righteous (Psalm 119:137), holy (Isaiah 54:5), and just (Revelation 16:5). His ways—His actions and commands—naturally reflect His nature of rightness, purity, and justice. When we follow in His ways, it is natural that it "produces this kind of fruit in our lives: love, joy, peace, patience, kindness, goodness, faithfulness, gentleness, and self-control" (Galatians 5:22–23). When we follow in God's ways, we experience the fruit of his Spirit, which enables us to enjoy God's protection and provision.

Seeing God's Protection

It was a warm, dark night, and Justin and his girlfriend Maddie wanted to go swimming. Justin knew that the neighbors down the street were away for an extended time, and they had a beautiful in-ground pool in their backyard. So he and Maddie sneaked behind the neighbor's house, scaled the fence surrounding the pool, and set out to enjoy an evening swim.

Justin threw off his shoes, climbed the diving board ladder, and before Maddie could even get her shoes off, dove in. He heard her scream just before he lost consciousness.

The neighbors had drained most of the water from the pool, leaving only a few feet in the deep end. Unable to see this in the darkness, Justin's dive ended with a shallow splash of water and a sickening crunch of bones. His late-night dive paralyzed him from the neck down for the rest of his life.

This couple wanted nothing more than to enjoy the pleasure of a twosome swim party. The fence marked a boundary—a boundary that implicitly said, "Do Not Enter," "No Trespassing," and "Keep Out." But Justin saw the fence as a killjoy meant to keep him and his girlfriend from having the fun they wanted. In reality, however, the fence was meant for his protection.

Communicate clearly and often to your kids that the boundaries God has given us are placed there for their protection. His laws and instructions are there to protect them spiritually, emotionally, relationally, and physically. God has even given us guidelines to protect our physical health. Over forty years ago, Dr. S. I. McMillen wrote a brilliant book called *None of These Diseases*. He demonstrated how over two dozen divine commands or standards found in the Bible served to prevent such disorders as heart disease, cervical cancer, and arthritis long before the advent of modern medicine! Dr. McMillen wrote in the preface:

> *When God led the Israelites out of afflicted Egypt, he*
> *promised them that if they would obey his statutes,*
> *he would put "none of these diseases" upon them.*
> *God guaranteed a freedom from disease that modern*
> *medicine cannot duplicate.*[1]

That doesn't mean if we always obey God we'll never get sick. But God's commandments do act as a protective boundary between us and the consequences of wrong choices. They function much like an umbrella. When we put up an umbrella, it shields us from the rain. But if we choose to move out from under that umbrella during a storm, we're bound to get wet. As long as we and our families stay under the umbrella of God's commands, we'll be shielded from many negative consequences. If we step out from under that protective cover, however, we should not be surprised if we suffer the negative effects of our wrong choices.

Seeing God's Provision

Committing to God's ways does protect us from many negative consequences in life. But protection is only one side of the coin. The other side is provision. Following God's ways not only protects us, it also provides us with our deepest needs.

God told Abraham to take his son Isaac to Mount Moriah and sacrifice him as a burnt offering. Abraham was in the process of following God's command when an angel of the Lord said, "Don't lay a hand on the boy!" (Genesis 22:12). Isaac was spared, and God provided Abraham with a ram as a substitute sacrifice. After Abraham offered the sacrifice, he "named the place Yahweh-Yireh (which means 'The LORD will provide')" (Genesis 22:14).

Notice the future tense of the name's meaning. You would think Abraham might have referred to God as the one who *did* provide, since the ram was provided to meet an immediate need and not a future one. But instead, he chose the term, "Jehovah-Jireh"—the God who *will* provide—because God not only provides for the moment; He also provides for the future.

God is both our provider and protector. Throughout history He has provided for His children and protected them. In his psalms, King David consistently pictured God as the great provider and protector. Notice Psalm 145 in particular:

> *The LORD always keeps his promises; he is gracious in all he does.*
> *The LORD helps the fallen [protector] and lifts those bent beneath the loads [provider].*
> *The eyes of all look to you in hope; you give them food as they need it [provider].*
> *When you open your hand, you satisfy the hunger*

and thirst of every living thing [provider].

The Lord is righteous in everything he does; he is filled with kindness.

The Lord is close to all who call on him, yes, to all who call on him in truth [protector].

He grants the desires of those who fear him [provider]; he hears their cries for help and rescues them [protector].

The Lord protects all those who love him [protector]. (Psalm 145:13–20)

Everything you have and everything you will have as God's child—materially, physically, emotionally, relationally, and spiritually—is from Jehovah-Jireh, the provider God. Jesus said to "Seek the Kingdom of God above all else, and live righteously, and he will give you everything you need" (Matthew 6:33). Living a godly life sets us free to be what God intended us to be and enjoy life as He designed.

When Jesus said, "You will know the truth, and the truth will set you free" (John 8:32), He spoke of a dual freedom. Adhering to the truth of God not only gives us freedom *from* the destructive consequence of such things as lying, cheating, stealing, jealousy, hatred, sexual immorality, etc. We also receive freedom *to* participate in the positive aspects of loving God and others when we are being faithful and pure, patient and kind, giving and generous. Such godly living reaps the rewards of trusting and secure relationships, deepened friendships, a good reputation, etc. As we follow in God's ways, we are freed *from* harm and freed *to* enjoy the benefits of right choices.

Communicating God's Provision and Protection

To solidify the reality of God's protection and provision, it helps to point out actual instances in which making the right moral choice provides a positive benefit and prevents a negative consequence. Let's say, for example, that your daughter has just purchased a five-dollar tube of lipstick at a store. She gives the clerk a ten-dollar bill, and as she counts her change she realizes that the clerk has accidently given her a twenty-dollar bill instead of the five-dollar bill she intended. Your daughter hesitates; she could really use the extra money. But after considering the choice, she does the right thing and returns the twenty to the grateful clerk.

This is a teachable moment for you, her parent. When your child makes the choice to be honest when it might seem more advantageous to do otherwise, be sure to point out the benefits of protection and provision her choice brings to her.

What are some of the protections and provisions that come from honesty?

Protects from	Provides for
Guilt	A clear conscience
Shame	A sense of accomplishment
A cycle of deceit	A reputation for integrity
Ruined relationship	Trust

Make a big deal of it when your kids perform positive acts, such as showing respect for authority or giving honor to a teacher or an elder by their courteous attitude and speech. Or if your kids refuse to join in as others make fun of a student that has a disability or one who is a little odd, make a point of commending them for it. Point out how showing respect to others. . .

Protects from	Provides for
Harming Relationships	Healthy relationships
Being offensive	Attractiveness
Receiving condemnation	Approval

Identifying to our kids the provision and protection of right moral choices reinforces the positive benefits of following in God's ways. In our *Right from Wrong* book, we covered eight values or commands of God and outlined twenty-nine ways we are protected and provided for when we live them out. (Learn more about the *Right from Wrong* book in the epilogue.)

There is good reason the apostle Paul admonished all of us to "Run from sexual sin!" (1 Corinthians 6:18). It is in our best interest to follow God's guidelines in our sex lives. Paul went on to say:

> *You can't say that our bodies were made for sexual immorality. They were made for the Lord, and the Lord cares about our bodies. . . . Run from sexual sin! No other sin so clearly affects the body as this one does. For sexual immorality is a sin against your own body. (1 Corinthians 6:13, 18)*

Living sexually pure not only honors God, it honors our own bodies. There are significant benefits to following God's commands to live sexually pure and remain faithful to a present or future marriage partner. Here are a few of what we are protected from and provided for when we live sexually moral lives. Share them with your kids.

Protects from	Provides for
Guilt	Spiritual rewards
Unplanned pregnancy	Optimum atmosphere for child raising
Sexually transmitted diseases	Peace of mind
Sexual insecurity	Trust
Emotional distress	True intimacy
Broken relationships	Loving relationship

I made a choice early on not to engage in sexual activity until I could do it in the context of the loving commitment of marriage. Because Dottie and I entered our marriage relationship as sexually pure partners, we have been protected from feelings of guilt and have enjoyed an uninterrupted relationship with God.

We have never had to go through the heartache of an unplanned pregnancy. Consequently, our children, conceived within a loving married relationship, have had the opportunity to be raised by their biological mother and father.

We have been protected from the fear that any sexually transmitted disease might come into our marriage bed.

We have been protected from the sexual insecurity that can occur from being compared to past sexual lovers one's spouse may have had. Consequently, we have experienced the provision of trust in our relationship.

We have been protected from the emotional distress that premarital sex can bring and the feelings of betrayal that an extramarital affair can cause. As a result, we have enjoyed relational intimacy unobstructed by breaches of trust or ghosts from the past. Following God's instructions in terms of purity and faithfulness in our human relationships brings glory to God and blessings to us.

We realize that not everyone has remained sexually pure prior to marriage or faithful during marriage. That does not mean that all is lost. It is important for those who have made these mistakes to know that God is faithful and forgiving, and He can restore broken hearts, broken emotions, and broken marriages. Michael Leahy, author of *Porn Nation*, is just one example of this kind of restoration. His marriage was completely destroyed through his addiction to pornography. When he hit rock-bottom in his life, he turned to God. Through God's love, forgiveness, and healing power, Michael was fully restored. Today he travels across the country speaking to college students about the dangers of pornography and the power of God's redemptive grace.

The negative consequences of pornography have been proven to be extremely damaging. Ongoing research shows that an individual's continued use of internet pornography is a predictor for

- Marital distress, separation, and divorce.
- Decreased sexual satisfaction.
- Decreased sexual intimacy.
- Infidelity.
- Overspending, debt, and decreased job security.[2]

In addition, current studies find that the frequency of porn viewing correlates with

- Depression.
- Anxiety.
- Stress.
- Less sexual and relational satisfaction.

- Altered sexual tastes.
- Poorer quality of life and health.
- Real-life intimacy problems.[3]

I have traveled away from home for most of my married life. I have had many opportunities to view porn in various venues, including the internet. But I have developed this deep conviction: any momentary thrill that porn provides is no match for the lasting fulfillment that God provides when I follow His ways of faithfulness and purity. Resisting temptation and remaining faithful to God and Dottie has paid off in so many ways. Dottie tells me that my commitment to purity deepens her sense of worth as my wife, gives her security, and tells her she is loved. Knowing that we keep ourselves solely for one another increases our relational intimacy. Our commitment to faithfulness and purity in our relationship gives us a powerful real-life example to share with our kids and grandkids.

Take advantage of your own story to teach your kids the benefits of faithfulness and purity. There is no such thing as a perfect marriage, so use the mistakes and failures as illustrations as well. We don't have to be perfect to be effective models of how to make right choices.

Allow me to end as we began. King David wrote, "The foundations of law and order have collapsed. What can the righteous do?" (Psalm 11:3). In the next verse, he answered his own question: "The LORD still rules from heaven. He watches everyone closely, examining every person on earth" (Psalm 11:4).

In Deuteronomy 6:6–7, God said, "Commit yourselves wholeheartedly to these commandments that I am giving you today. Repeat them again and again to your children. Talk about them when you are at home and when you are on the road, when you are going to bed and when you are getting up."

We parents are given the exalted privilege of revealing to our kids the nature of our loving and awesome God. He instructs us to explain to them everything about His ways that protects them from harm and provides for them a life of meaning, fulfillment, and joy—not just for this life, but for all eternity.

We can fulfill this responsibility by teaching our kids to consider their moral choices, compare them to God, commit to living in God's ways, and then count on God's protection and provision. No, it's not easy. And our kids won't always make the right choices. But, I repeat, with God's help and a few effective tools, we can instill God's moral values in our kids to "live clean, innocent lives as children of God, shining like bright lights in a world full of crooked and perverse people" (Philippians 2:15).

In the epilogue, we provide you with some added tools to help you on your journey to raise up a generation who can be set free to choose right.

EPILOGUE

Resources That Can Help

*Y*ou need all the help you can get when it comes to raising up a generation to make right moral choices. Surround yourself with good resources and other parents and friends who want to help their own kids choose right.

We have referenced the fact that this book is a companion to the 1994 *Right from Wrong* book. While the book is over twenty years old, the values and truth it presents are still relevant today. You can take advantage of this book by going to www.thomasnelson .com/right-from-wrong.

Want to help your preteens and teens gain a better grasp of a God who has their best interest at heart? Introduce them to *#Truth—365 Devotions for Teens Connecting Life and Faith*. This daily devotional will inspire and challenge your kids to consider their choices, compare them to God, and commit to His ways. Check it out at www.barbourbooks.com.

Get your church involved in addressing the right from wrong message. We have created a free "Set Free to Choose Right" sermon and a special article specifically for your pastor. Check out the "Choose Right Church Pack" at www.josh.org/set-free -journey.

What is unique about this church pack is that men, women, and teens have the ability to receive a series of free short two-minute videos through a smartphone. Following the pastor's sermon on how to make right choices, he can offer men, women, and teens a Set Free Journey of 14–21 equipping video messages.

These are designed to help you become a more powerful person of grace to those struggling with internet porn.

In fact, you can access the Set Free Journey right now. If you're a man simply text "set free" to 33733. For you ladies, text "set free her" to 33733. And for teens, text "set free yth" to 33733.

In watching these short messages, you will notice there are links below each video. They are links to resources, specifically designed to help a person break free from the grips of porn use. There is also information on finding Christian counselors trained in helping those struggling with this issue.

It is important to acknowledge that we need one another in our efforts to set our young people and others free to make right moral choices. We need the support and accountability of our friends and family. To make accountability and loving support a reality within your family and the church, check out the amazing service available through *Covenant Eyes* at www.covenanteyes .com.

You can equip your kids to make right moral choices for life. You can help them know why right is right and wrong is wrong. You can be that person of grace that can help empower them to choose right over wrong.

The apostle Paul gives us a fitting close to this book:

> *A final word: Be strong in the Lord and in his mighty power. Put on all of God's armor so that you will be able to stand firm against all strategies of the devil. For we are not fighting against flesh-and-blood enemies, but against evil rulers and authorities of the unseen world. . . . Therefore, put on every piece of*

God's armor so you will be able to resist the enemy in the time of evil. Then after the battle you will still be standing firm. (Ephesians 6:10–13)

Exhibit

=====

Excerpts From

The Porn Phenomenon

THE IMPACT OF PORNOGRAPHY IN THE DIGITAL AGE

A Barna report produced in partnership with
Josh McDowell Ministry

1. The Landscape of Porn

"I know it when I see it." So said Supreme Court Justice Potter Stewart when he was asked to define pornography.

His oft-quoted statement demonstrates a perennial problem: It is notoriously difficult to define pornography. What counts as sexually explicit material is both highly subjective and highly contested—especially considering recent and rapid shifts both in pornography's form (that is, the media used to create and deliver it) and its function (people's reasons for producing or viewing it).

The word "pornography" is a combination of two Greek words: *pornē*, meaning "prostitutes," and *graphein*, "to write about." In ancient times, pornography was not images but words.

A modern cultural understanding of pornography started with words too. It began to emerge when the first erotic novels were published in Victorian-era England.[1] These books spun tales of sexual exploits intended to sexually arouse the reader and, shortly after they were published, pornography was criminalized by the British Parliament in the Obscene Publications Act of 1857.[2] According to the law, content alone does not make pornography of words or images. An equally important element is the *function* of the content—that is, the purpose intended by the creator, adopted by the user, or both.

This definition created two required components of pornography: *form* and *function*. The 1857 law thus codified the first culturalized understanding of pornography. And though form has evolved significantly since the nineteenth century, the notion of function remains important for today's understanding of what counts as pornography.

Why does this matter? Because if you're like many leaders, your first impulse is to be concerned with content (form) rather than function. But a person's intentions toward sexually explicit content are a more pressing matter. Certainly, blocking access to content can be helpful as a first step for a person who wants to be free from porn use. But, as we will hear from our expert contributors, the heart—the desires and longings that lie deep within—must be transformed if the person is going to experience true freedom.

What Is Porn?

How do Americans define pornography? While nearly everyone agrees that "an image of sexual intercourse" is definitely porn, the issue of function seems to be at the center of most people's thinking. If you use it for masturbation or personal arousal, it's porn. Simple as that.

Most of us have probably been to an art museum or taken an art history class in which we saw a fully nude statue or painting. You probably didn't consider that pornography, and most Americans agree with you. Less than one-quarter of adults over age 25 (24%) consider a fully nude image to be objectively pornographic.

But if that fully nude image is sexually arousing, that's a different story. Half of adults over age 25 (53%) say that "a fully nude image that is sexually arousing" is definitely pornography. It is the second-highest defining factor in the younger age groups, with nearly 7 in 10 young adults (69%) and 8 in 10 teenagers (78%) agreeing.

When asked what is "definitely porn," teenagers and young adults are more likely than older adults to consider any of the options to be pornography. This may come as a surprise. One might assume that, having grown up in a hypersexualized culture where nude images and sexual situations are part of everyday life, younger Americans might have become sexually desensitized. But it seems such desensitization takes time—curiosity and the "forbidden" nature of sex may play a role in teens and young adults feeling as if more content is risqué.

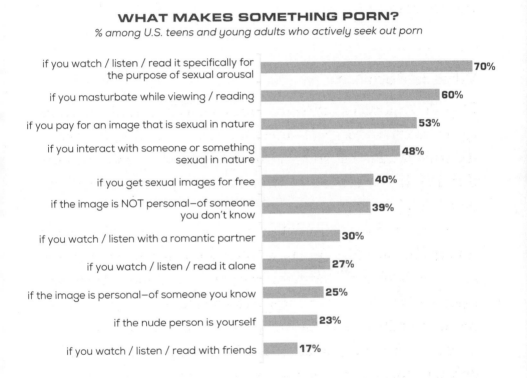

WHAT MAKES SOMETHING PORN?
% among U.S. teens and young adults who actively seek out porn

if you watch / listen / read it specifically for the purpose of sexual arousal	70%
if you masturbate while viewing / reading	60%
if you pay for an image that is sexual in nature	53%
if you interact with someone or something sexual in nature	48%
if you get sexual images for free	40%
if the image is NOT personal—of someone you don't know	39%
if you watch / listen with a romantic partner	30%
if you watch / listen / read it alone	27%
if the image is personal—of someone you know	25%
if the nude person is yourself	23%
if you watch / listen / read with friends	17%

For many people, it's not just the user's intent that defines something as pornographic, but also the producer's intent. More than 8 out of 10 adults 25 and older indicate an image is porn if it is comprised of "sex scenes that make up most or all of a video, with very little story" (84%); two-thirds consider a "still picture of sexual acts" to be pornography (66%); and 6 in 10 consider "close-up still pictures of genitals" to be porn (61%). Teens and young adults report similar views, but are again somewhat more likely to put many of the options in the porn category.

The context of a sex scene also matters a great deal to people's perceptions. A lack of narrative seems to indicate to most teens and adults that the primary purpose of the scene is to arouse the viewer—and therefore, is porn. On the other hand, "sex scenes that are a short part of a broader story" are considered pornographic by just two in five adults (22%) and 3 in 10 teens and young adults (31%). If a sex scene is integral to a story, most Americans do not consider it pornography.

The genesis of pornography—the written word—still counts as porn for some Americans. 3 in 10 adults (30%) and 4 in 10 teens and young adults (41%) consider sex scenes described in a written story to definitely be porn. The massive popularity of the *50 Shades of Grey* novels lends credibility to this idea.

IMAGES & ACTIVITIES THAT ARE *DEFINITELY* PORN

% among U.S. teens, young adults and adults 25+ who actively seek out porn

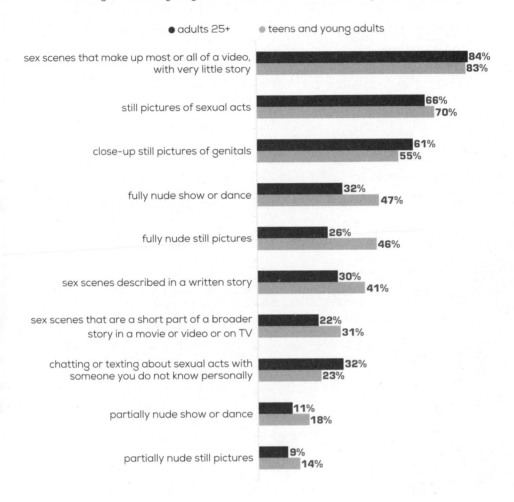

● adults 25+   ● teens and young adults

Category	adults 25+	teens and young adults
sex scenes that make up most or all of a video, with very little story	84%	83%
still pictures of sexual acts	66%	70%
close-up still pictures of genitals	61%	55%
fully nude show or dance	32%	47%
fully nude still pictures	26%	46%
sex scenes described in a written story	30%	41%
sex scenes that are a short part of a broader story in a movie or video or on TV	22%	31%
chatting or texting about sexual acts with someone you do not know personally	32%	23%
partially nude show or dance	11%	18%
partially nude still pictures	9%	14%

Special Report: Porn 2.0

The cavalier attitude of most teens and young adults toward porn, coupled with accessibility created by technology, is pushing pornography into a new era that is more social, interactive, dynamic and personal. The majority of teens and young adults (63%) report receiving a nude image from someone else via text, email, social media or app. Among those who have received a nude image, 58 percent say it was sent by their boyfriend or girlfriend and 21 percent say it was sent by a friend. More rarely the nude image was sent through a group of friends (3%).

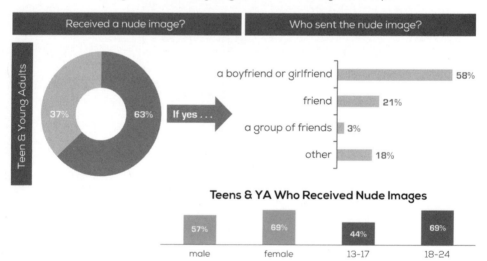

TEENS & YOUNG ADULTS WHO HAVE RECEIVED NUDE IMAGES

% among U.S. teens and young adults who actively seek out porn

Received a nude image? / Who sent the nude image?

Teen & Young Adults

37% / 63% / If yes . . .

a boyfriend or girlfriend — 58%
friend — 21%
a group of friends — 3%
other — 18%

Teens & YA Who Received Nude Images

male 57% / female 69% / 13-17 44% / 18-24 69%

Compared to the two-thirds who have received a nude image, just 40 percent of teens and young adults have *sent* such images to someone via text, email, social media or app. Because there are fewer senders than receivers, it is likely that senders tend to send images to more than one person. Senders most often send images to their boyfriend or girlfriend (75%), which may indicate that sexting is becoming an accepted practice of dating culture. It also may explain why young adults are more likely than teens to send and receive nude images: They have greater freedom to date around when they're not living at home.

Compared to men, women more often receive (69% vs. 57%) and send (51% vs. 33%) nude images via text, email, social media or app. The reasons for this gender disparity are unclear and more research is needed to explore the social pressures or lack of inhibition young women experience related to sexting.

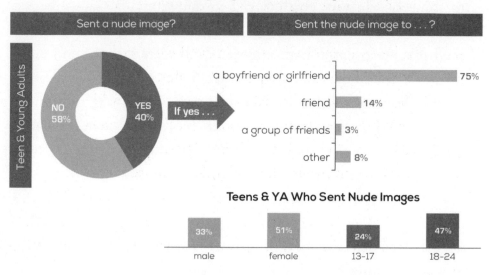

TEENS & YOUNG ADULTS WHO HAVE *SENT* NUDE IMAGES

% among U.S. teens and young adults who actively seek out porn

Sent a nude image?

Sent the nude image to . . . ?

Teen & Young Adults

NO 58%

YES 40%

If yes . . .

a boyfriend or girlfriend — 75%

friend — 14%

a group of friends — 3%

other — 8%

Teens & YA Who Sent Nude Images

male	female	13-17	18-24
33%	51%	24%	47%

Smartphone cameras are now ubiquitous and are connected directly to the online universe; social networking sites allow for the exchange of these images; and the genre of "amateur," "reality," and "voyeur" porn has enticed many to utilize these technologies to broadcast themselves in what has become a frenzied, chaotic, and impossible-to-control pornographic landscape.[3]

Among teens and young adults, sexting and sharing explicit images through social media apps like Snapchat and Instagram have become commonplace. However, minors who send or receive sexual images often do not recognize the serious social, legal, emotional, and psychological risks of doing so—particularly in cases where images are shared without consent.[4] In which case, things can go horribly wrong:

> Jesse Logan, an eighteen-year-old high school senior from Ohio, sent a nude photo of herself to her boyfriend, who then made the decision to forward it to four other girls. The photo went viral, and Jesse was ostracized by her peers and quickly spun into an emotional depression. Taunted and labeled a "slut," a "whore," and a "porn queen," Jesse Logan hanged herself at her home a few months later.[5]

Another case demonstrates the complexities involved when the students are minors:

> In the winter of 2010 in Lacey, Washington, a fourteen-year-old named Margarite took out her cell phone and snapped a full-length photo of herself, naked, in her bathroom mirror. She then sent the photo to a potential new boyfriend, Isaiah, at his suggestion. A few weeks later, Isaiah forwarded the photo to another eighth-grade girl, a former friend of Margarite's, who transmitted it (along with the text "Ho Alert!") to dozens of others on her cell phone contact list. Margarite became instantly (in)famous in her middle school; other kids began calling her a "slut" and a "whore," and she received sneers and ogles from peers she barely knew. Her friends were ostracized for associating with her. School officials

soon discovered the situation, and the police were notified. Reaction was swift: the county prosecutor chose not to press charges against Margarite herself, but three students involved in the case, including Isaiah and two of the girls who forwarded Margarite's photo, were charged with distributing child pornography—a Class C felony. All these students were in eighth grade.[6]

Attempts to curb the crisis of sexting and "self-pornification" have generally taken three forms: "prosecutorial, pedagogical, and technological."[7] Cases like the one involving Margarite have set out to prosecute sexting as a criminal offense. Educators are attempting to create awareness of the dangers of sexting. And tech companies are writing software that allows parents to monitor the cyber-life of their children.[8] But some argue these strategies rely too heavily on worst-case scenarios and will, in the end, be as effective (or ineffective) as similar campaigns against drug use. "A more sophisticated approach requires an examination of the forces that compel teenagers to share these images in the first place."[9]

What motivates young people to participate in sexting when the consequences can be so severe? Obvious answers include a desire to flirt or gain popularity, to meet the requests or demands of a significant other, and to explore and express sexuality in a playful but not-yet-actualized sexual activity. But this is an incomplete picture. Teen sexting takes place within a larger system where teens replicate broader social behavior.[10]

Self-pornification is a result of teens and young adults coming of age in an increasingly pornified American culture that "encourages and rewards the pornographic impulse. Take the examples of self-pornographers like Kim Kardashian, Pamela Anderson, and Paris Hilton, all of whom have been generously rewarded for their public displays of private moments."[11]

> When adolescents are taught, largely through the mass media, that sexual experience is a desired good, and these values are then perpetuated among their peers, it seems clear that portraying oneself as sexual would be a desirable strategy.[12]

In American popular media and advertising, women's bodies are routinely sexualized and objectified. These images promote the message that a woman's identity and worth depend heavily on how physically attractive and sexy she appears.[13] It's not hard to imagine that these cultural messages contribute to the sexting phenomenon. But these aren't the only messages young people receive. "Their superiors—teachers, parents, legislators, and law enforcement agents—expect from them a degree of moral purity and ethical exactitude that is demanded from no other social group."[14]

> The message of purity culture is, ironically, not so different from our overly sexualized popular media culture: for both, a woman's worth lies in her ability, or her refusal, to be overtly sexual. Both approaches teach American girls that their bodies and their sexuality are what make them valuable.[15]

The sexting crisis embodies the contradictions and complications teens face in a world that is pulling them in opposite directions. And dealing with the epidemic of sexting must take into account these complexities. Approaches must send a strong message of deterrence that includes not only the dangers and consequences of sexting, but casts a vision for identity and sexuality that challenges pornified popular culture.

Talking about Porn

As any parent or youth pastor can tell you, the teen and young-adult years are characterized by sexual discovery and identity formation—and much of that work is done in the company of peers. It is therefore unsurprising to find that more than one-quarter of 13- to 24-year-olds talk to their friends about porn, either often or occasionally (28%). Young adults (34%) talk about porn more often than their teenage counterparts (18%). Heading off to college and breaking away from parental supervision may create conditions for greater freedom to discuss and explore sexual topics. (The fact that half of young adults estimate that "all" or "most" of their friends regularly look at porn, compared to only one-third of teens, supports this case.) Peer evaluation, guidance, and approval are a more prominent part of life in young adulthood. As such, discussions about porn may more easily become part of everyday interactions.

Predictably, young men (36%) report talking about porn with their friends more often than young women (20%). This may be because men look at porn more often than women—at least, that seems to be the general assumption among teens and young adults. (It's also true.) Twenty-two percent say men view porn most often; 42 percent say "mostly men and a few women" consume pornography; and about one-third say porn consumption is split evenly between the sexes (33%).

Among those who talk with friends often, occasionally or seldom about pornography, most do so in a way that is either accepting (36%) or neutral (42%). An additional 16 percent talk with their friends about porn in a positive or lighthearted way, with no one expressing shame for having viewed it. Teens and young adults generally assume that most people look at porn at least on occasion, and the morality of porn is rarely discussed or even considered. Just 1 in 10 teens and 1 in 20 young adults report talking with their friends about porn in a disapproving way.

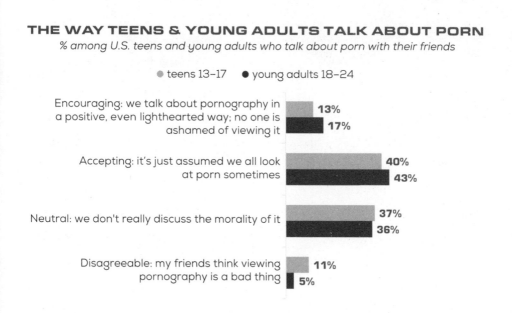

THE WAY TEENS & YOUNG ADULTS TALK ABOUT PORN
% among U.S. teens and young adults who talk about porn with their friends

● teens 13–17   ● young adults 18–24

Encouraging: we talk about pornography in a positive, even lighthearted way; no one is ashamed of viewing it	13% 17%
Accepting: it's just assumed we all look at porn sometimes	40% 43%
Neutral: we don't really discuss the morality of it	37% 36%
Disagreeable: my friends think viewing pornography is a bad thing	11% 5%

These somewhat cavalier attitudes make sense when one considers young people's assessment of porn's prevalence among their friends. Half of young adults (49%) and one-third of teens (32%) say all or most of their friends regularly view porn.

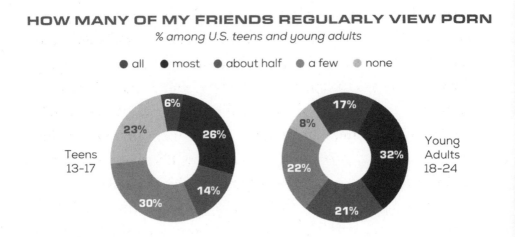

HOW MANY OF MY FRIENDS REGULARLY VIEW PORN

% among U.S. teens and young adults

● all   ● most   ● about half   ● a few   ● none

Teens 13-17

6% · 26% · 14% · 30% · 23%

Young Adults 18-24

17% · 32% · 21% · 22% · 8%

2. The Uses of Porn

How often do people view porn?

This is not an easy question to answer. Living in a hypersexualized and pornified media culture means that catching sight of explicit images requires little effort. People often come across images they never intended to see through online newsfeeds, pop-up advertisements, emails, texts, search engines, billboards and signs, and many more inputs. A constant stream of images vying for your attention means that "viewing" requires extra thought—an intent—to actually focus on and *see* the image. Without this kind of focused attention, sexually charged images are like driving by a forest: You know you're passing trees but, if you don't stop and take a look, your brain only registers a blur of green.

Consequently, rather than asking how often people "view" porn—a general and vague measure of porn use—Barna created a way to triangulate data related to seeing porn and a person's *intention* to view porn. As previously discussed, the intent behind viewing an image is critical for determining whether an image is considered porn. Applying this reasoning to frequency of views, researchers parsed the data based on a person's intent.

To measure frequency of porn use in the United States, Barna asked a nationally representative panel ages 13 and older (1) how often they "come across" porn, even if they are not seeking it out, and (2) how often they "actively seek out" porn.

Of men 25+, 65 percent come across porn at least once or twice a month, with 25 percent less often than that. Forty-seven percent of these men seek it out at least once or twice a month with another 19 percent seeking it out less often. Only 10 percent of men 25+ say they never seek out porn.

Among women 25+, 34 percent come across porn at least once

or twice a month, with 42 percent less often than that. Twelve percent of these women seek it out at least once or twice a month with another 16 percent seeking it out less often. Seventy-three percent of women 25+ say they never seek it out.

Coming Across vs. Seeking Out

Smartphones, tablets, and laptops have revolutionized the way we encounter images; pictures and videos are easily accessible with one swipe or click. The ubiquity of online pornography, coupled with open and unlimited access to information and imagery through new media and technology, are key reasons people stumble onto pornography on a regular basis. It doesn't take much effort to encounter sexually explicit content on apps like Snapchat and Instagram, or even via text messaging (some of which is unsolicited).

Pornified images in mainstream media, including in video games, increase a person's chances of encountering sexually explicit material. Popular culture is awash in sexualized images and ideas; you only need to see an Axe commercial, Miley Cyrus performance, or "reality" show like *The Bachelor* for confirmation.[16]

The "pornification" of pop culture is, at least in some ways, the byproduct of a broader cultural shift against authority and objectivity, particularly in youth culture, that manifests in self-expression, subjectivity, and experimentation.[17] The normalization of porn is creating a hypersexualized culture in which younger generations are now coming of age. They, in turn, tend to be more open to sexual experimentation and self-expression—leading to further social acceptance of sexually explicit content. It's unclear where (or if) this self-perpetuating feedback loop will end.

The more frequently a person consumes pornography online or through internet-connected apps, the more he or she is targeted through ad networks that use cookies—little packets of data on his or her device that track online activity and browsing history and then share that information with advertisers and retailers. The more porn a person consumes, the more invitations he or she receives to consume porn.

The data clearly shows that the more frequently a person actively seeks porn, the more frequently he or she will come across porn—even when he or she is not actively searching for it. Researchers cross-referenced how frequently someone comes across porn with how often someone seeks it out—*and found a direct correlation*. If a person seeks out porn on a daily basis, he or she is more likely to come across porn on a daily basis. The same goes for those who seek out porn weekly, once or twice a month, and less often.

Porn Use by Age

When it comes to running across porn, as opposed to actively seeking it out, the differences between teens (ages 13 to 17), older Millennials (25 to 30) and Gen-Xers (31 to 50) are statistically insignificant. However, the percentage among young adults 18 to 24 is significantly higher than other age segments. Since actively searching for porn increases one's chances of coming across porn—and young adults are more likely than others to seek it out—this result is as expected.

Young adults may also come across porn more frequently than other age cohorts because they tend to have more "comprehensive" notions of what qualifies as porn. This may seem counterintuitive, but in four out of five scenarios young adults are more likely than older adults to classify an image as porn. Consequently, when people of different ages see the same image, the younger person is a bit more likely to perceive the image in question as porn.

Porn Use by Faith Practice

Under Barna's definition, *practicing Christians* are self-identified Christians who agree strongly that their faith is very important in their life and have attended a church worship service within the past month. (Self-identified Christians who do not meet these criteria are called *non-practicing Christians.*) Practicing Christians report coming across porn somewhat *less* frequently than other Americans. Just 9 percent of practicing Christians, for example, come across porn on a daily basis compared to 14 percent among the rest of the population. Likewise, 17 percent of practicing Christians say they come across porn weekly, compared to 23 percent among those who are not practicing Christians.

Besides the obvious explanation—that practicing Christians seek porn less often than others, and so come across it less often—porn-blocking filters, which make it less likely for a device user to unintentionally stumble across porn, are also more common among practicing Christians. Seventeen percent who have sought out porn in the past report installing such filters on all their devices, compared to only 11 percent among all adults who have ever searched for porn.

Practicing Christians do, indeed, seek out porn much less frequently than other teens and adults. Just 2 percent search for porn daily, compared to 8 percent of other Americans; 5 percent search weekly, compared to 17 percent among the rest of the population; and 6 percent seek out porn once or twice a month, compared to 17 percent of all others. Seven in 10 practicing Christians (72%) report never searching for porn, compared to 39 percent of those who do not practice Christianity.

Barna researchers wondered which factor of practicing faith (if any) has a greater impact on how frequently one seeks out porn: (1) church attendance or (2) having a faith that is important to one's life. It turns out that infrequent church attendance is not a significant factor when it comes to porn use. A low-priority faith, however, *is* strongly correlated with more frequent porn seeking. In fact, self-identified Christians who do not consider their faith important are *more likely than the national average* to seek out porn daily, weekly, and once or twice a month.

Why People Use Porn

How often do people view porn? is an important question. Even more important, however, is *why* they view it. As discussed in the previous chapter, function takes precedence over form. Without recognizing the reasons that compel people to use pornography— regardless of how often they use it—it's impossible to know what spiritual, relational or emotional needs lie at the root of their compulsion.

With this in mind, let's examine the reasons people say they use porn, and look at some of the differences between groups.

The most common reason among both teens and adults is *personal arousal* (62%). Other top reasons include "curiosity" (31%), "it's just fun" (29%), "to get tips or ideas for my own sex life" (28%), "boredom" (25%) and "to set the mood with a spouse / girlfriend/boyfriend/partner" (24%). (There are significant generational differences that we'll explore, as well.)

REASONS PEOPLE SEARCH FOR PORN

base: U.S. teens and adults 13 and older who have ever actively sought out porn (multiple response)	% total
for personal arousal	63
curiosity	33
it's just fun	30
to get tips or ideas for my own sex life	29
boredom	27
to set the mood with a spouse / girlfriend / boyfriend / partner	24
it's less risky than actually having sex	15
to express my sexuality	14
no particular reason	5
haven't thought about it	3
because my friend(s) do(es)	1

Among those who view porn for personal arousal, 13 percent actively seek it out on a daily basis, 29 percent do so weekly, 33 percent once or twice a month, and 26 percent less often. The majority searches for porn weekly or monthly (62%).

There is a high correlation between frequent use and doing so for personal arousal. Among those who seek out porn on a daily basis, 76 percent do so for personal arousal. Among those who search weekly, 72 percent do so for personal arousal. And among those who seek it out once or twice a month, 71 percent do so for personal arousal.

Those who search for porn because "it's just fun" are more

likely to view porn on a daily basis (54%). Somewhat similarly, "to express my sexuality" is most common among those who use porn daily (24%) or weekly (20%), but less so among those who do so once or twice a month (5%) or less often (6%).

Ministering to the Whys

Consider how you and your faith community address porn use. How well do you focus on the *reasons* different people use it and tailor your ministry approach accordingly? For example, since teens and young adults often cite "boredom" as their reason for seeking porn, is it possible there is a spiritual gap in their lives? Perhaps they do not know how to be quiet, able to rest and enjoy God's presence in stillness. Training Christians in the spiritual disciplines of prayer and silence is something the Church has done for centuries—can your church do the same for the young people in your community, so they can be free of the restlessness that prompts them to fill every second with distraction?

Or consider the single adults in your church who may use porn as "substitute sex" out of loneliness. Do they have the deep connections they need to know they belong in God's family? Are the couples and families in your church making room for singles in their home lives?

Each person in your congregation or faith group who uses porn, no matter how much they use, does so for a reason. The road to wholeness and freedom begins with finding out their *why*.

3. Porn & Morality

Freedom of conscience, enshrined in the First Amendment to the US Constitution, is deeply rooted in the nation's DNA. The earliest colonists left Europe in search of religious freedom and their descendants codified protections against religious tyranny in the country's founding documents.

Americans cherish the right to believe whatever they wish—which turns out to be a mixed blessing. For example, reaching consensus around a moral code for society is difficult when no one can agree on the source or arbiter of that code.

Most of our cultural forebears looked to a higher being as the ultimate source of moral knowledge and the final moral authority. But recent Barna research shows that today's Americans are more prone to turn inward for such knowledge. Half of all US adults believe that "ethics and morals are based on what seems right to a person based on their own judgment and ideas" (53%). Nine out of 10 believe "people should not criticize someone else's life choices" (89%) and 8 out of 10 say "people can believe whatever they want, as long as those beliefs don't affect society" (79%). This inward-oriented search for truth or purpose also leads 9 out of 10 adults to agree "the best way to find yourself is by looking within yourself" (91%) and 86 percent to say "to be fulfilled in life, you should pursue the things you desire the most." When it comes to the sexual expression of that desire, nearly 9 out of 10 Americans believe "each person has to decide his or her own sexual boundaries" (88%).

In other words, the only moral code most people agree on is that each person is the sole moral authority for himself. Each individual must decide for himself what is right and wrong, taking into account his needs, desires, hopes, and dreams. In their book *Good Faith*, David Kinnaman and Gabe Lyons call this the *morality of self-fulfillment.*[18]

Accounting for society's allegiance to this moral code is essential for understanding attitudes toward pornography in the US today. Not only is there a lack of consensus on the moral goodness or badness of porn, but there are also myriad views about its impact on society. These are largely based on how porn is perceived to be or not to be a source of self-fulfillment—because self-fulfillment is the final word on morality in today's culture.

Keeping in mind the underlying assumption that self-fulfillment is a moral nonnegotiable, let's take a look at how US teens and adults view the morality of porn.

Porn on the Scales of Morality

Teens, young adults, and adults 25 and older rated a series of action statements according to a five-point scale: "always OK," "usually OK," "neither wrong nor OK," "usually wrong" and "always wrong." Combining the percentages of those who chose always and usually wrong for each statement, a picture emerges of where using porn ranks on a list of possible immoral actions.

The short answer? Low.

Barely half of adults say viewing porn is wrong (54%) and it ranks only seventh on a list of 11 actions—behind overeating (58%), which is #4.

ACTIONS THAT ARE WRONG: ADULTS 25+

base: adults 25 and older	% usually + always wrong
1. taking something that belongs to someone else	95
2. having a romantic relationship with someone other than a spouse	89
3. saying something that isn't true	87
4. overeating	58
5. wanting something that belongs to someone else	57
6. thinking negatively about someone with a different point of view	55
7. viewing pornographic images	54
8. reading erotic or pornographic content (no pictures)	46
9. not recycling	44
10. significant consumption of electricity or water	39
11. watching sexually explicit scenes on TV or in a movie	37

Teens and young adults are roughly 10 points less likely than older adults to think each of the actions is wrong. In addition, the ranking order below the top three are quite different between the younger and older age cohorts. (It is not necessarily surprising that the two groups agree on these top three actions as always or usually wrong, since all three have legal consequences to greater or lesser degrees—and the leap from *illegality* to *immorality* is a small jump for most people. When it comes to actions on which the rule of law has no say, however, the two age cohorts rank them quite differently with respect to immorality.)

Actions that may negatively impact the environment rank higher among teens and young adults than among older adults. The younger group has grown up in the age of climate change, manmade natural disasters, droughts, mandatory recycling, electric cars, pesticide-free farming, and so on. Thus it is not surprising that they perceive a moral dimension to actions with environmental implications. (It is notable, however, that "not recycling" ranks so highly.)

ACTIONS THAT ARE WRONG:
TEENS & YOUNG ADULTS 13 TO 24

base: teens and young adults 13–24	% usually + always wrong
1. taking something that belongs to someone else	88
2. having a romantic relationship with someone other than a spouse	75
3. saying something that isn't true	71
4. not recycling	56
5. thinking negatively about someone with a different point of view	55
6. overeating	48
7. significant consumption of electricity or water	38
8. wanting something that belongs to someone else	32
9. viewing pornographic images	32
10. reading erotic or pornographic content (no pictures)	27
11. watching sexually explicit scenes on TV or in a movie	24

Older adults seem to retain a greater vestige of Judeo-Christian morality than younger Americans. For example, "overeating" (58%) and "wanting something that belongs to someone else" (57%) are both sins according to Christian tradition: gluttony and covetousness. Nearly 6 in 10 adults 25 and older say these actions are immoral, compared to just half of teens and young adults who say overeating is wrong (48%) and one-third who believe coveting is wrong (32%).

The moral code of self-fulfillment is alive and well in both age groups. "Thinking negatively about someone with a different point of view" is perceived to be always or usually wrong by more than half of teens and young adults (55%) and adults 25 and older (55%). The highest moral good is not figuring out what is right, but accepting each person's view as "right for them."

For most teens and young adults, using porn seems to fall into this category. Only one-third believes viewing pornographic images is always or usually wrong (32%), compared to more than half of older adults (54%). About one-quarter says reading erotic content (27%) or watching sexually explicit TV or movie scenes (24%) is immoral.

There appears to be a momentous generational shift underway in how pornography is perceived, morally speaking, within our culture—at least when it comes to each person choosing for himself whether to use porn. Yet when it comes to assessing porn's impact on society more broadly, people are more apt to hold a negative view.

Which presents an interesting paradox of belief: Porn is fine for individuals but bad for society.

Special Report: Pastors & Porn

1 IN 5 YOUTH PASTORS AND 1 IN 7 SENIOR PASTORS USE PORN.
THAT'S MORE THAN 50,000 US CHURCH LEADERS.

*W*hen they think about US Protestant pastors as a group, nearly two-thirds of the pastors Barna interviewed say porn use is a major (6%) or significant (58%) problem among these leaders—but it's not the most pressing problem. About three-quarters say burnout (79%), marital problems (78%), or pride (73%) are bigger problems than porn use, and two-thirds say finances (65%) and disagreements among the church leadership (64%) outweigh porn as difficult issues pastors are dealing with.

Rather than only asking pastors about "pastors" as a macro group, researchers also asked church leaders about themselves. (All surveys were anonymous.) One in five youth pastors (21%) and one in seven senior pastors (14%) admitted they currently use porn. About half do so at least a few times per month, and the vast majority feels guilt or shame when they do so. More than half of youth pastors who use porn (56%) and one-third of senior pastors who use porn (33%) believe they are addicted.

Porn use by any church leader is a problem, but senior pastors' responses are cause for particular concern. Senior leaders are more likely than their youth leader counterparts to say that their job makes it easy to use porn in secret and that neither their spouse nor even a trusted friend is aware of their struggle. There also seems to be a tendency among senior leaders to underestimate or downplay the impact of porn use both on their ministry and on their relationships. And although a majority says they feel guilt or shame related to their porn use, senior pastors are less likely than youth leaders to say so.

These data combine to paint a portrait of senior leaders in isolation, too many of them unaware of or in denial about the spiritual and relational risks they are running—risks that have the potential to harm not only themselves but others. In recent years we have seen ample evidence that, for some pastors and priests, the spiritual power they wield can too easily lead to sexual coercion and abuse. If, as some experts suggest, porn is implicated in sexual violence, the Christian community and its leaders must bring these struggles into the light.

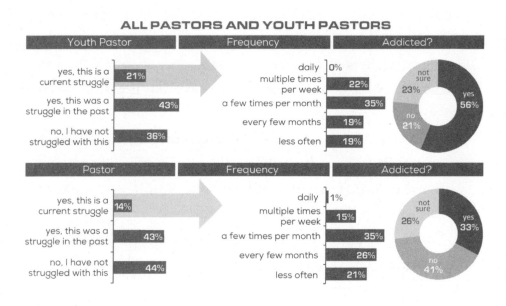

ALL PASTORS AND YOUTH PASTORS

Youth Pastor		Frequency		Addicted?
yes, this is a current struggle	21%	daily	0%	not sure 23%
yes, this was a struggle in the past	43%	multiple times per week	22%	yes 56%
no, I have not struggled with this	36%	a few times per month	35%	no 21%
		every few months	19%	
		less often	19%	

Pastor		Frequency		Addicted?
yes, this is a current struggle	14%	daily	1%	not sure 26%
yes, this was a struggle in the past	43%	multiple times per week	15%	yes 33%
no, I have not struggled with this	44%	a few times per month	35%	no 41%
		every few months	26%	
		less often	21%	

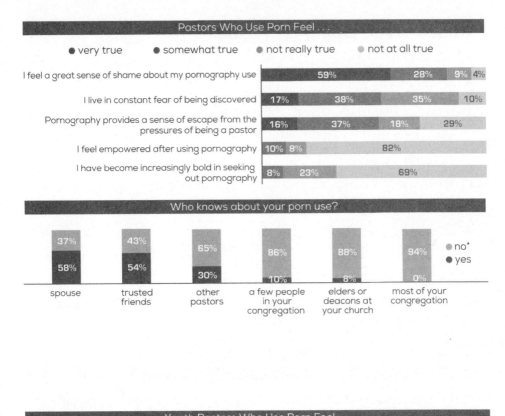

Pastors Who Use Porn Feel . . .

● very true ● somewhat true ● not really true ● not at all true

	very true	somewhat true	not really true	not at all true
I feel a great sense of shame about my pornography use	59%	28%	9%	4%
I live in constant fear of being discovered	17%	38%	35%	10%
Pornography provides a sense of escape from the pressures of being a pastor	16%	37%	18%	29%
I feel empowered after using pornography	10%	8%	82%	
I have become increasingly bold in seeking out pornography	8%	23%	69%	

Who knows about your porn use?

● no* ● yes

	spouse	trusted friends	other pastors	a few people in your congregation	elders or deacons at your church	most of your congregation
no*	37%	43%	65%	86%	88%	94%
yes	58%	54%	30%	10%	8%	0%

Youth Pastors Who Use Porn Feel . . .

● very true ● somewhat true ● not really true ● not at all true

	very true	somewhat true	not really true	not at all true
I feel a great sense of shame about my pornography use	62%	32%	3%	3%
Pornography provides a sense of escape from the pressures of my role	22%	22%	12%	45%
I live in constant fear of being discovered	18%	38%	27%	18%
I have become increasingly bold in seeking out pornography	4%	11%	28%	57%
I feel empowered after using pornography	3%	24%	73%	

Who knows about your porn use?

● no* ● yes

	trusted friends	spouse	other pastors	girlfriend / boyfriend	elders or deacons at your church
no*	22%	29%	52%	64%	80%
yes	75%	72%	46%	36%	14%

*The third option was "not sure."

What We Are Doing for Pastors

Barna asked self-identified Christians 25 and older what they think should be done if a church finds out its pastor is using porn. Two out of five (41%) think the pastor should be fired or asked to resign. Three in 10 say he should take a leave of absence until he stops (29%). Combined, that's seven out of 10 Christians who say a pastor should leave ministry, at least for the time being, if he is found to be using porn.

It may be that these are the right courses of action for a church, but it is also understandable, given these responses, why pastors might be inclined to hide their porn use at all costs. It is also important to acknowledge a serious—and unbiblical—double standard: One in five of those who say the pastor should resign (20%) and one in four who say he should take a leave of absence (27%) actively seek porn for themselves at least occasionally.

For their part, only 8 percent of pastors say a pastor struggling with porn should resign. Instead, he should find a professional counselor (82%) or a group of mature Christians who can hold him accountable (59%) and, if married, tell his spouse (58%).

Q&A with Marlene Soffera

Pastor, speaker, writer

Rev. Marlene Soffera is a minister ordained by the Church of God (Anderson). She has served local congregations as an associate pastor and as a lead pastor, and serves the wider church as a speaker at retreats and conferences. Marlene cofacilitates a weekly LIFE Ministries support group for wives of sex addicts, and leads workshops for clergy and lay leaders on the topic of pornography addiction. Marlene and her husband of 42 years, Greg, live in California.

Q: You colead a support group for wives of sex addicts. In your experience, what are the most common relational effects of porn use? What do you hear from women about the effects of their husband's sex addiction?

A: The breakdown of trust is the number-one issue reported by wives of sex addicts. This is true no matter the form in which their husband's addiction manifests itself, all the way from "simple" use of pornography to extramarital affairs (often with the wife's friends or relatives), prostitutes, rape, pedophilia, etc. Every one of these activities is shrouded in secrecy and layers of lies and broken promises. When the lies finally come to light, usually in a dramatic discovery, the wife's trust in her husband is almost completely shattered. It is a very long and difficult process to rebuild trust.

Second, a husband's addiction often creates huge self-esteem problems for his wife. A woman tends to compare herself unfavorably to the virtual women in her husband's life. She instinctively feels that she does not measure up. She is not enough in and of herself to satisfy her spouse, so her self-esteem takes a nosedive. On top of that, many a sex-addicted husband tells his wife about the many ways in which she is inadequate, actually blaming her for his addiction: "I wouldn't *need* pornography if only you. . .had bigger boobs / were thinner / wore your hair differently / were more aggressive sexually / were more passive sexually / wore this costume." The wife is left feeling worthless, guilty, and shameful. Wives age, and simply cannot compete with enhanced pornographic females who are perpetually in their teens and early twenties.

A third damaging issue is a lack of intimacy, both emotionally and (often) physically. At its core, sexual addiction is an intimacy disorder. The addict often struggles to achieve a genuine emotional intimacy with his wife, often because of childhood wounds. He finds it much easier to bond with a virtual wife / sex partner because there is no need for relational give and take. There's just *take*. Perhaps surprisingly, sex addicts also often struggle with physical intimacy. A husband can't control the outcome of a sexual encounter with his wife in the same way he can when "engaging" just with himself. Many addicts deprive their wives of sexual encounters because: (1) They have difficulty achieving an erection or otherwise "performing" without the constant visual stimulation pornography provides, and (2) they have already "spent" themselves (sometimes several times a day) with their pornographic "partners." There is simply nothing left to give to their wives. Because of this emotional and physical distance, wives of sex addicts often feel very alone.

These three issues contribute to anger and depression in the wife, and often lead to separation and divorce. This goes on to affect generations of children and grandchildren. Pornography use and abuse is not a victimless crime. It is a crime against the whole family.

Q: Only about 1 in 11 churches has a program specifically designed to help people who are struggling with porn use. When about one-third of practicing Christian men and teen boys report seeking porn at least once a month, any ideas about why so few churches offer support within the worshipping community? What would you tell leaders who want to offer something but aren't sure where to start?

A: A number of Christian-based recovery groups for pornography/sex addicts are designed to be led by recovering addicts. They are not programs that "just anyone" can effectively lead. Church boards don't simply decide to start such a ministry like they might vote to start a food pantry or bus ministry. It's like Alcoholics Anonymous. It requires a leader to be transparent enough to say, "I'm a recovered sex addict, and I want to start a chapter affiliated with such-and-such ministry." That kind of vulnerability can come at a huge cost. Will the church leadership throw the guy off the board if he admits to that kind of sinful past or ongoing struggle? Will they "de-Christianize" him? If that man starts the group and promotes it to the congregation, will the laity shun him for his less-than-holy thoughts and actions? If that man is the pastor, will the church fire him for being a sex addict? Sex and sex addiction is a touchy subject in the church, shrouded in mystery, misunderstanding, and a great deal of shame. Offering support within the worshipping community requires a very brave, committed, and *recovering* leader who is willing to suffer negative consequences in order to provide healing and hope to others. Many congregations simply do not have a person who is sufficiently recovered to lead, or sufficiently brave to be that vulnerable.

If church leadership feels led to address the issue but doesn't have a qualified leader at hand, they can still find a path to ministry. That path begins with research. A simple internet search for Christian sex addict recovery groups will yield several options to explore, such as L.I.F.E. Ministries, Covenant Eyes, etc. These groups have lots of resources, and can often direct people to a recovery group in their community or a nearby city. The pastor could inquire at the city's ministerial association to see if some other congregation already has such a support group in place. These groups are usually very willing to accept "outsiders" into their group. It is not unusual for one denomination to start and host a support group that ends up with participants from many different denominations. Each separate church can promote and support the work of the church that started the ministry. (It's called being the *Church!*)

Q: Looking at the Barna findings, what (if anything) stands out to you as encouraging, and why? What (if anything) do you find discouraging, and why?

A: Encouraging: the fact that more and more people are approaching their pastor or youth pastor for help with their pornography issues.

Discouraging:

- Porn use is considered amoral or is increasingly accepted.
- A significant minority of respondents do not consider nonconsensual sex acts to be "always wrong."

- Women's use of pornography is on the rise.

Increasing acceptance of pornography use will lead to increasing levels of actual sex addiction. Any, even slight, trend in the direction of normalizing nonconsensual sex acts contributes to a worsening of our current rape culture. And women's increasing use of pornography will lead them into addiction just as it does for men, and the consequences will be equally devastating. The effects of a woman's addiction on her husband are just as devastating as a husband's addiction on his wife. All the issues of trust, self-esteem, intimacy, anger, depression, and so on are the same when the tables are turned.

Q: In your experience, how does life stage play a role in someone's motivations for porn use? How, if at all, does that change your approach to, say, teens and young adults from your approach to married, older adults?

A: The Barna research shows that people across the age spectrum use porn "for personal arousal" along with boredom, curiosity, fun, etc. The reality *for the addict*—differentiated from a more casual user—is that porn is their drug of choice to medicate the pain of past wounds (often these are "father wounds," and that's why I recommend therapy to get to the core of the problem). Few middle-aged people who don't already drink, do drugs, or use pornography suddenly decide to start using. Rather, people usually choose how to deal with pain at a young age. While alcohol and drugs are most common, pornography is rising rapidly—and most young people do not even realize it is "medication." Curious teens or twentysomethings (or even children) are hooked long before they know the "why" of their woundedness. We need to address the issue with teenagers and point them in the direction of healing before that happens. Unfortunately, the challenge is how to do that with the awareness, full acceptance, and consent of their parents.

For married, older adults, we're not dealing with new users, but people who have ingrained behaviors and corresponding issues. My approach is as I mentioned above: recovery groups, individual counseling, and marriage counseling. It is extremely rare to hear of a miraculous prayer cure for an addict.

Chapter 1

[1] The Porn Phenomenon Study, commissioned by the Josh McDowell Ministry with research conducted by the Barna Group, 2016, 66.

[2] Barna Research, "The End of Absolutes: America's New Moral Code." Research released in Culture & Media article, May 25, 2016, Barna.org.

[3] Ibid.

[4] Duke Pesta, "Moral Relativism and the Crisis of Contemporary Education," The New American.com, December 1, 2011, http://www.thenewamerican.com/culture/education/item/372-moral-relativism-and-the-crisis-of-contemporary-education.

[5] Josh McDowell and Bob Hostetler, *Right from Wrong* (Nashville, TN: Thomas Nelson Publishers [previously Word Publishing], 1994), 265.

[6] Professor Robert Sapolsky, "Dude, Where's My Frontal Cortex?" *Nautilus Biology/Neuroscience*, July 24, 2014, http://nautil.us/issue/15/turbulence/dude-wheres-my-frontal-cortex.

[7] Ibid.

[8] John Monterosso and Barry Schwartz, "Gray Matter: Did Your Brain Make You Do It?" *New York Times Sunday Review*, 27 July 2012, Opinion Page, Neuroscience and Moral Responsibility.

[9] "Teens Look to Parents More Than Friends," *Science Daily*, June 15, 2011, http://sciencedaily.com/releases/2011/06/110615120355.htm.

[10] Ibid.

[11] Jeffrey Rosenberg and W. Bradford Wilcox, "The Importance

of Fathers in the Healthy Development of Children," publication of US Department of Health and Human Services, 2006, http://childwelfare.gov/pubs/usermanuals/father-hood/fatherhood.pdf.

[12] "Talking to Your Teen about Sexuality," publication of Hillsborough County University of Florida Extension, http://hillsborough.ifas.ufl.edu/documents/pdf/fcs/A-Z_family/sexuality.pdf.

Chapter 2

[1] The Porn Phenomenon Study, 2016, 84–85.

[2] Ibid, 25.

[3] Barna Research, "The End of Absolutes: America's New Moral Code." Research released in Culture & Media article, May 25, 2016, Barna.org.

[4] Ibid.

[5] Jacob Poushter, "What's Morally Acceptable? It Depends on Where in the World You Live," PewResearchCenter, April 15, 2014, http://www.pewresearch.org/fact-tank/2014/04/15/whats-morally-acceptable-it-depends-on-where-in-the-world-you-live/.

[6] Ibid.

[7] Drawn from Josh McDowell, Sean McDowell, 77 *FAQs about God and the Bible* (Eugene, OR: Harvest House Publishers, 2012), 64–65.

[8] Ibid., 61.

Chapter 3

1 Lenny Savino, "Suspect's Letter Gives Hijackers Instructions," *Akron (Ohio) Beacon Journal*, 29 September 2001, A1, A5.

Chapter 4

1 The Porn Phenomenon Study, 2016, 28.

2 Ibid., 29.

3 Karen Peterson-Iyer, "Mobile Porn?: Teenage Sexting and Justice for Women," *Journal of the Society of Christian Ethics* 33, no. 2 (Fall/Winter 2013): 93.

4 Belinda Luscombe, "Porn and the Threat to Virility" *Time Magazine*, 11 April 2016, 42.

5 Victor Cline, "Pornography's Effects on Adults and Children," September 27, 2009, accessed January 2016, http://www.scribd.com/doc/20282510/Dr-Victor-Cline-Pornography-s-Effects-on-Adults-and-Children#scribd.

6 Joan Atwood, *The Effects of the Internet on Social Relationships: Therapeutic Considerations* (Bloomington, IN: iUniverse, 2011), 165–66.

7 Ibid.

8 Drawn from Josh McDowell *10 Commitments for Dads* (Eugene, OR: Harvest House Publishers, 2014), 21–22.

Chapter 5

[1] The Porn Phenomenon Study, 2016, 41.

[2] Dr. Ted Roberts as quoted during the Josh McDowell Ministry/ Covenant Eyes hosted Set Free Summit on Tuesday, April 5, 2016, in Greensboro, NC.

[3] The Porn Phenomenon Study, 2016, 81.

[4] Dr. Ted Roberts as quoted April 5, 2016, Greensboro, NC.

[5] The Porn Phenomenon Study, 2016, 112.

[6] Ibid., 109.

[7] Jayson Graves of Healing for the Soul as quoted during the Josh McDowell Ministry/Covenant Eyes hosted Set Free Summit on Tuesday, April 5, 2016, in Greensboro, NC.

[8] The Porn Phenomenon Study, 2016, 83.

[9] Ibid., 83.

[10] Ibid., 118.

[11] Kendra Cherry, "What is Brain Plasticity?" VeryWell, June 14, 2016, https://www.verywell.com/what-is-brain-plasticity-2794886.

Chapter 6

[1] The Porn Phenomenon Study, 2016, 84–85.

[2] Ron DeHaas, Founder and CEO of Covenant Eyes, quoting the Barna Group research analysis during the Josh McDowell Ministry/Covenant Eyes hosted Set Free Summit on Wednesday, April 6, 2016, in Greensboro, NC.

[3] Ibid.

[4] Ibid.

[5] Ibid.

[6] Ibid.

Chapter 7

[1] The Porn Phenomenon Study, 2016, 41.

[2] Charles Darwin, *The Descent of Man and Selection in Relation to Sex* (New York, NY: Penguin Books, republished in 2004), 91.

[3] Ibid., 91.

[4] Adapted from Josh McDowell and Thomas Williams, *The Relational Word* (Holiday, FL: Green Key Books, 2006), 24–25.

Chapter 8

[1] Drawn from Chapter 11 of Josh and Dottie McDowell's *Straight Talk with Your Kids about Sex* (Eugene, OR: Harvest House Publishers, 2012), 39–41.

Chapter 10

[1] S. I. McMillen, *None of These Diseases* (Westwood, NJ: Spire Books, 1968), preface.

[2] Vivian Chan, MC, RCC, "The Impact of Pornography on Marital Relationships," The Wishing Wells, January 11, 2009, http://www.wishingwellscounselling.com/family/the-impact-of-pornography-on-marital-relationships/.

[3] Gary Wilson, *Your Brain on Porn* (Margate, Kent England, Commonwealth Publishing, 2014), 34.

Exhibit

[1] David Foxon, *Libertine Literature in England, 1660–1745* (Fort Lee, NJ: Lyle Stuart, 1965), 45; see also H. Montgomery Hyde, *A History of Pornography* (London: Heinemann, 1969), 14.

[2] *Obscene Publications Act of 1857* (20 & 21 Vict. c.83).

[3] Dennis Carlson and Donyell L. Roseboro, eds., *The Sexuality Curriculum and Youth Culture* (New York: Peter Lang Publishing, Inc., 2011), 349.

[4] Karen Peterson-Iyer, "Mobile Porn?: Teenage Sexting and Justice for Women," *Journal of the Society of Christian Ethics* 33, no. 2 (Fall/Winter 2013): 93–110.

[5] Ibid., 94.

[6] Ibid., 93.

[7] Carlson and Roseboro, *The Sexuality Curriculum*, 350.

[8] Ibid.

[9] Ibid., 355.

[10] Peterson-Iyer, "Mobile Porn?"

[11] Carlson and Roseboro, *The Sexuality Curriculum*, 350.

[12] Bruce E. Drushel and Kathleen German, *The New Pornographers: New Media, Sexual Expression, and the Law* (New York: The Continuum International Publishing Group, 2011), accessed January 2016, http://www.academia.edu/510376/The_New_Pornographers_New_Media_Sexual_Expression_and_the_Law.

[13] Ibid.

[14] Carlson and Roseboro, *The Sexuality Curriculum*.

[15] Peterson-Iyer, "Mobile Porn?," 100.

[16] Lisa Myers, "The Pornification of Popular Culture: The Normalization of Sex through Popular Music and Social Media," *Movable Type*, accessed January 2016, http://movabletypeuva .com/the-pornification-of-popular-culture/.

[17] Ibid.

[18] David Kinnaman and Gabe Lyons, *Good Faith: Being a Christian When Society Thinks You're Irrelevant and Extreme* (Grand Rapids, MI: Baker Books, 2016).

Josh McDowell has been at the forefront of cultural trends and groundbreaking ministry for over five decades. He shares the essentials of the Christian faith in everyday language so that youth, families, churches, leaders, and individuals of all ages are prepared for the life of faith and the work of the ministry. This includes leveraging resources based on years of experiences, new technologies, and strategic partnerships. Since 1961, Josh has delivered more than 27,000 talks to over 25,000,000 people in 125 countries. He is the author or coauthor of 142 books, including *More Than a Carpenter* and *New Evidence That Demands a Verdict*, recognized by *World Magazine* as one of the top 40 books of the twentieth century. Josh's books are available in over 100 different languages. Josh and his wife, Dottie, are quick to acknowledge that after their love for the Lord, family is their greatest joy and top priority. They have been married for 46 years and have four wonderful children and ten beloved grandchildren. For more information, please visit www.josh.org.

IF YOU LIKED THIS BOOK, YOU'LL LIKE...

#Truth
by Josh McDowell

This daily devotional from Josh McDowell unpacks spiritual truths that inspire, challenge, and fuel young people every day of the year—from January 1 to December 31. Practical and relevant, each month of devotional readings shares a common theme—from January: THE TRUTH THAT GOD EXISTS to December: THE TRUTH ABOUT CHRIST'S RETURN.

Paperback / 978-1-63409-975-2 / $16.99

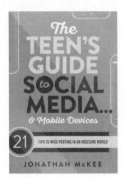

The Teen's Guide to Social Media and Mobile Devices
by Jonathan McKee

Jonathan McKee shares helpful tips for today's teens and tweens navigating the digital world. With tips like *Nothing you post is temporary* and *Don't post pics you wouldn't want Grandma, your boss, and Jesus seeing! (Jesus is on Insta, you know!)*, Jonathan's approach is refreshingly honest and humorous, as one who knows teens and understands the way they think, providing information for them to make informed decisions and challenging them in a way that encourages and inspires without belittling.

Paperback / 978-1-68322-319-1 / $12.99